The Genealogy of the Mickley Family of America

Together With a Brief Genealogical Record of the Michelet Family of Metz, and Some Biographical Sketches and Historical Memorabilia

By Minnie Fogel Mickley

Published by Pantianos Classics

ISBN-13: 978-1-78987-655-0

First published in 1893

Contents

Preface .... *iv*

Introduction .... *vi*

Of the European Ancestry of the Mickleys 11

The Michelet Family 14

The American Branch of the Mickley Family 18

Genealogy of the Mickley Family 20

War Record 43

European Genealogy 46

Joseph J. Mickley - A Biographical Sketch by His Friend J. Bunting 53

Obituaries 66

Historical Memorabilia 77

    II - Extracts From Pennsylvania Archives 78

Indexes 81

    Index First 81

    Index Second 87

To my honored friend and relative, the philosopher, Dr. Charles Louis Michelet, and to the memory of John Jacob Mickley, and his descendants, these pages are respectfully dedicated by his great, great, great granddaughter,

The Compiler.

THE COAT OF ARMS OF THE FAMILY MICHELET.

MOTTO— WAR, THE CHASE AND LIBERTY.

Preface

It has taken a long time to present the Genealogy of the Mickley Family of America to the descendants of John Jacob and Elizabeth Barbara Burkhalter.
Thanks are due to many members of the family who have rendered invaluable assistance, and to the Rev. J. D. Schindel, Mrs. E. P. Allbrecht and Mile. Julia M. Beerstacher for translations from the French and German.

The Rev. J. Marion Mickley, Mrs. Maria and Mrs. Kate Mickley Comfort and Daniel W. Mickley, all of Adams County, Pennsylvania, have given me interesting data concerning their ancestor, John Martin Mickley, and the family of Mrs. Hannah Mickley Fackenthall gave me valuable information concerning their ancestor, John Peter Mickley, of Bucks County, Pennsylvania.

The family Bibles of the different families have been the chief source of information, and the work has been put in order in the same style as the Loomis Genealogy compiled by Professor Elias Loomis, Yale College.

Enough data has been gathered of the Deshler family to compile a Deshler Genealogy, which, it is our hope, to furnish at a future time.

The amount of labor involved in such a compilation can be estimated only by those who have attempted similar work. It would have been disheartening but for the great pleasure it has afforded me to endeavor to preserve the records of our family and give them a permanent form.

Minnie Fogel Mickley.

Mickleys, 1893.

Note — It will be observed in the genealogical record that, in many instances, the date is wanting. Any one who may be able to supply this missing information or any other touching the family record, will confer a favor by forwarding the same to the compiler, addressed to Mickleys, Pa.

Introduction

Joseph J. Mickley, in the preface of his "Brief Account of Murders by the Indians and the Causes Thereof, in Northampton County, Pennsylvania, October 8th, 1763," read by him at a reunion of the family, has the following:

"A large number of the descendants of John Jacob Mickley (the first of that name in America) assembled on the farm, formerly his property, in North Whitehall Township, Lehigh County, where the Indians murdered two of his children, and also the family of John Schneider, on the adjoining farm, the 8th of October, 1763. In commemoration of that event, the following paper was prepared and read, October 8th, 1863. At that time I had no intention of publishing the same, but having been repeatedly urged by some of my relations and several esteemed friends, finally concluded to have it printed; it may however, be of little or no interest, except, perhaps, to some of the numerous descendants of our ancestor, John Jacob Mickley.

"In connection with this, it may not be out of place, and acceptable to some, to give such information of our ancestors as has been handed down to us, partly from documents, and partly by tradition. Traditional accounts, however, though generally based on some truths, become, in course of time, very much distorted and augmented, so that not much reliance can be placed on them unless supported by documentary evidence; therefore some part of my statement about our ancestors may require correction. Bancroft says, very justly: 'Memory is an easy dupe, and tradition a careless story-teller.'

"From what I have been able to gather, it appears that our family is descended from French Huguenots, the name having originally been written Michelet, but corrupted, and variously written Miquelet, Miickli, etc., and finally Anglicized into the present form, Mickley; that during the persecution of the Huguenots in France, they emigrated to the bordering Dukedom of Deux Fonts (Zweibrücken), then a part of the German Empire; where they were unmolested in the exercise of their religion.

"I have not been able to ascertain whether our ancestor, John Jacob, or any other of them, was born in Deux Ponts. When, during my visit there in the year 1869, the records were examined at my request, I felt very much disappointed in being told that nothing could be found to show that such a family had ever resided in that country; and, if ever existed there, it must have been recorded in that office, but that record is now lost.

"It may not be surprising that the records are missing, after the enactment of such stringent laws against the Huguenots during the reign of the French King Louis XIV. For instance, the edict of 1681, which, deprived them of nearly all their civil rights; the imperious order given to burn all their books; and the revocation of the Edicts of Nantes, October 22d, 1685. In the burning of their churches and books, probably all their church records shared the same fate with the general destruction, excepting such as may have been carried out of the country by the refugees. To this may be added that, through the devastation of the Palatinate and other German provinces by the French in the reign of the same King Louis XIV, many valuable documents were irretrievably lost.

"We have, however, authentic information that our ancestor, John Jacob Mickley, was born in Europe, in the year 1697; that he came to America in the ship Hope, of London, from Rotterdam, Holland, arriving in Philadelphia, August 28th, 1733. He was married in this country to Elizabeth Barbara, daughter of Ulrich Burkhalter, and settled in Whitehall Township, Northampton Count", now North Whitehall, Lehigh County, and died in August, 1769. He left three sons and two daughters, viz.:

"John Jacob, the eldest, my grandfather, who settled on a tract of land bordering on the village of Hokendauqua, in South Whitehall, Lehigh County; he had six sons and four daughters. A number of his descendants still reside in that county.

"John Martin, the second son, who was in the battle of Germantown, sold the old homestead, and moved to and settled in Adams County, near Gettysburg, in the year 1794. He had four sons and live daughters. Many of his descendants are living in different parts of that county.

"John Peter, the third and youngest son, of whose escape from the Indians, an account is given on the following pages, was in the military service against the Indians, and in the War of the Revolution, during the whole time of its continuance, in the capacity of fifer. He was in the battle of Germantown. At the close of the war he married, and settled in Bedminster Township, Bucks County, about the year 1784. He had two sons and eight daughters. Some of his descendants are still living in Bucks County, and one daughter, Mrs. Statzell, eighty-eight years of age (yet very active), besides other descendants, are living in Philadelphia.

"One daughter of John Jacob Mickley, the first, became the wife of Andrew Miller, who resided in Linn Township, Lehigh County. She had no children.

"The other daughter was married to Peter Deshler, of Whitehall Township. By him she had three sons and one daughter. After the death of Deshler, she married Michael Bieber, of Allen Township, in Northampton County. She had no children by Bieber.

"In preparing this account about the Indians, I have drawn from the most reliable authorities, and rejected many incredible verbal stories about Indian affairs which had been added in course of time, so that the statements may be tolerably correct. I cannot omit to express my great satisfaction in having visited John Peter Mickley, in Bucks, and his sister, Mrs. Bieber, in Northampton County, in the year 1819, and obtained many facts from them in relation to this matter; whatever the one related to me, was corroborated by the other. From them I also learned that the 8th of October, 1763, was one of those clear, pleasant days which have frequently been experienced at that time of the year. Owing to the occurrence of the Indian murders, that day has always been mentioned by our family as the beginning of Indian Summer."

In closing the account, he says:

"When the condition of this part of the country is considered, in which, one hundred years ago, a few families were living, without protection, in a wilderness, deprived of almost every comfort, exposed to attacks from wild beasts and reptiles, and the danger of being murdered, and have their property destroyed by hostile Indians, who kept them constantly in such fear that the members of the families bade each other farewell in the evening before retiring, being under the impression that they might not meet again on the next morning; when such a melancholy state of affairs is compared with the present flourishing condition, where now the people are living in peace, themselves and property protected, and where are seen numerous finely cultivated farms, with convenient habitations, furnaces, manufactories, canals, railroads, improvements in every branch of industry, and the comforts of a numerous population; when all this is considered, we are impelled to profound gratitude. If any person exists who is unable to appreciate these advantages and blessings, he must be a heartless and ungrateful being, unworthy of living in this community.

"In the above I have presented such matter as I considered suitable on this occasion, and as might be agreeable to, at least, some of the descendants of our forefather, John Jacob Mickley. I shall be much pleased if by the facts here presented, sufficient interest has been excited in any one (more capable than myself) to pursue the subject further, and produce a more complete history of the Indian troubles at that time in this part of the country."

It is not within the limits of the present work to enter at any length upon the trials and hardships of our ancestors in their early frontier life; but the massacre of the Mickley children, October 8th, 1763, is of such deep interest to every member of the family that I quote in full the account as given by the late Joseph J. Mickley on the occasion of the One Hundreth Anniversary of the sad event:

"The approach of the Indians was seen by Ulrich Showalter, who was working on the roof of a building. The site being considerably elevated above the river Lehigh, he had a good opportunity to see and count the Indians. Twelve in all were seen wading across the river, a short distance above Siegfried's Bridge, to this day known as the "Indian Fall" or Rapids. The Indians crossed the river and landed near Leisenring's Mountain (now "Laurel Hill"). It is to be observed, that the greater part of this township was at that time still covered with dense forests, so that the Indians could go from one place to another almost in a straight line, through the woods, without being seen.

It is not known that they were seen by any one but Showalter until they reached the farm of John Jacob Mickley (No. 1), where they encountered three of his children, two boys and a girl, in a field under a chestnut tree gathering chestnuts. The children's ages were: — Peter, eleven; Henry, nine; and Barbary, seven; who, on seeing the Indians, began to run away. The little girl was overtaken not far from the tree by an Indian, who knocked her down with a tomahawk. Henry had reached the fence, and, while in the act of climbing it, an Indian threw a tomahawk at his back, which, it is supposed, instantly killed him. Both of these children were scalped. The little girl, in an insensible state, lived until the following morning. Peter, having reached the woods, hid himself between two large trees which were standing near together, and, surrounded by brushwood, he remained quietly concealed there, not daring to move for fear of being discovered, until he was sure that the Indians had left. He was, however, not long confined there; for, when he heard the screams of the Schneider family, he knew that the Indians were at that place, and that his way was clear. He escaped unhurt, and ran with all his might, by way of Adam Deshler's, to his brother, John Jacob Mickley, to whom he communicated the melancholy intelligence. From this time Peter lived a number of years with his brother John Jacob, after which he settled in Bucks County, where he died in the year 1827, at the age of seventy-five. One of his daughters, widow of the late Henry Statzel, informed me, among other matters, of a remarkable fact related by her father, namely: that the Mickley family owned at that time a very large and ferocious dog, which had a particular antipathy to Indians; and it was believed by the family, that it was owing to the dog the Indians did not make an attack on their house, and thus the destruction of their lives was prevented. John Jacob Mickley and Ulrich Flickinger, then on their way to Stenton's, being attracted by the screams of the Schneiders, hastened to the place where, a short time before, was peace and quietness, and saw the horribly mangled bodies of the dead and wounded, and the houses of Marks and Schneider in flames. The dead were buried on Schneider's farm."

The pamphlet of Joseph J. Mickley, (my great uncle), interested me very much, and led me to endeavor to gain more facts concerning our family history, in which I am pleased to say, I have been singularly successful. I gained a great deal of knowledge from my Uncle Joseph, my grand-father, Jacob Mickley, and my great aunt, Mrs. Andrew Sheldon, also from Prof. Dr. Charles Louis Michelet, the German Philosopher, who gave me interesting documents and authentic data.

My friendship and correspondence with Prof. Dr. Charles Louis Michelet, of Berlin, has been a great help to me in the preparation of this work. His interest in the family of America was such as to request of me a list of all the Mickleys of Pennsylvania, (descendants of John Jacob Mickley, 1697-1769).

In following the history of our family I am led to regard the influence of Suzane Mangeot, a Huguenot, as one of our greatest inheritances. It was through her influence Louis Michelet of Metz, became a Protestant, and as Huguenot Refugees, they were married in Zweibrücken, and their descendants in Berlin speak of themselves — not as "Berliners," but "Refugees."

The diary of Suzane Mangeot Michelet, is in the possession of Dr. C. L. Michelet of Berlin, and it was a great satisfaction to me to look through it, and I wish I could have read it through — as it would have given her descendants many interesting accounts of those troublous times after the revocation of the Edict of Nantes, during the times of the persecution of the Huguenots. Her eldest son, Jean Jacques, came to Pennsylvania in 1733, and was a worthy son of Huguenot refugees. He was one of the sturdy settlers of Whitehall Township, Pennsylvania, where, instead of religious persecution, he was tormented by wild beasts and Indians, and two of his children were massacred, as above narrated by J. J. Mickley, his great-grandson.

As a family, the Mickleys of America have led honest and upright lives — patriotic and useful, energetic and thrifty, not ambitious for office; no person of the name, to my knowledge, being a lawyer. Although some are physicians and ministers of the Gospel, the professions are not largely represented. Some are in the iron industry, and nearly all land owners and in comfortable circumstances. I have become acquainted, through my work, with a great many, and always found them ready to give me all the information I desired. As a rule they are very hospitable and trustworthy. During the Revolutionary War, John Jacob (No. 1) was entrusted with the removal of the bells of Philadelphia, bringing eleven of the bells, including Christ Church chimes and the State House bell, on his wagons and with his horses to Allentown, Pennsylvania, where they were concealed beneath the floors of Zion's Reformed Church, He was assisted by the Rev. Abraham Blumer, then Pastor of the church, whose son married Sarah, a daughter of John Jacob (No. 1).

They have always been active workers in the church, as the early records in Whitehall Township will show. Egypt, Mickleys, Allentown and Hokendauqua have in their first records the names of different members of the family. They belong mostly to the Reformed Church (which is the original Refugee Church of our forefathers) and the Presbyterian Church.

The family is not so widely scattered as would be supposed — although the name is represented in many of the States. California, New Mexico, Iowa, Minnesota, Kansas, Illinois, Maryland, New York, New Jersey, Ohio, Colorado and Pennsylvania are the homes of the Mickleys of America.

Prof. Dr. Charles Louis Michelet,
Berlin, Germany.

Of the European Ancestry of the Mickleys

From the following letters of Dr. C. L. Michelet, of Berlin, it appears that the descent of the American Mickleys from the Michelet, of Metz, is fully authenticated; but that prior to that date (1444), it is more or less conjectural,

I insert, however, Dr. Michelet's observations upon the history of the family as of the greatest interest and value:

"Berlin, April, 21st, 1883,
Buelow Street, 28,
S. W.

"Miss Minnie F. Mickley,

"*Esteemed Miss:* You will allow me to answer your English letter of the 9th of this month, in German, as I do not consider myself sufficiently competent to write a strictly correct letter in English, without some effort. You also, as the daughter of a German, no doubt understand this language.

"All the Michelets with whom I have any acquaintance come from Metz, and I have in my possession now a complete genealogical table of the family, dated from, the year 1444 up to the present day. This table is based for its truthfulness, partly, on the researches of the clergyman living there; partly, on the certificates of baptism belonging to the city, and partly on private papers belonging to my own immediate family.

"According to these researches, my great, great grandfather, Louis Michelet, was married in 1697 to Susanne Mangeot, whose diary, kept by herself, we have yet in good preservation, and in it she states she was married to her husband in Zwei-Brücken.

"I can now easily imagine why this betrothed couple was not married in Metz, because, on account of the revocation of the Edict of Nantes, 1685, no marriage was allowed to be solemnized, in the then French city, in accordance with the principles of the Protestant religion, and yet they were both secretly attached thereto. They went, consequently, to the neighboring Zwei-Brücken, in the Bavarian Palatinate, to celebrate their marriage, for since the peace of Westphalia, 1648, Germany had become friendly and co-equal.

"In the Statistical Archives of Metz is found, however, the information that Louis Michelet and his wife Susanne, in 1699, openly declared their adherence to the new religion, and that in 1715, Louis, now having become a widower, also declared his five children, Jean (John), Barbe, Marie, Louis (my great grandfather), and Pierre, as Protestants.

"What, however, I could not explain to myself in this connection was this: That, although the certificates of baptism of the last four children are jointly found in Metz, Barbe being born November 16, 1702; Marie, December 11, 1703; Louis (who emigrated to Berlin in 1720), December 8, 1705; Pierre, December 21, 1710; yet the certificate of Jean, the eldest, is entirely wanting, so that I even attached a mark of interrogation to his name in the genealogical table.

"Now, after what you communicate to me concerning your ancestor, John Jacob, this omission plainly explains itself. The married couple evidently remained yet awhile in Zwei-Brücken to await the birth of their first born.

"Should you desire to ascertain the exact date of birth of your ancestor, you would have to apply to the Protestant or Municipal Congregation of Zwei-Brücken, and request of it the authentic certificate of baptism of your Jean Jacques or Johann Jacob Michelet, stating such date of year as may be known to you.

"From all this, I believe that we may consider ourselves distant relatives, descending from two brothers, in about the fifth generation, and remain, with great respect.

Your devoted,
Prof. Dr. Michelet."

"Berlin, July 3d, 1883,
28 Buelow Street,
S. W.

"Miss Minnie F. Mickley,

"*Esteemed Miss:* The pamphlet of your great-uncle, as well as your letter of June 4th, I have just received. From the first I perceive that it would be almost hopeless to write to Zwei-Brücken for the purpose of obtaining transcripts of records concerning your ancestor, as during the plundering of the Palatinate, under Louis XIV, the French, no doubt, destroyed the Protestant documents there. Still, I would advise you to make the attempt.

"Nevertheless, it remains in the highest degree probable that your ancestor, John Jacob, was born and baptized as Jean, the son of Louis Michelet and Susanne Mangeot, in Zwei-Brücken. For I find in the whole Genealogical Tree, accompanying this letter, no other Jean who could have been born in 1697 or near that time. If I am correct in my opinion, then, according to the short genealogical table prepared by your great-uncle, my great grandfather, Louis, who was born in 1705 and went to Berlin in 1720, is the younger brother of John Jacob, the great grandfather of your grandfather and his brother, and I would then have, with both, the same great, great grandfather, Louis Michelet-Mangeot.

"It would also be quite natural that your grandfather, would be eight years older than myself, inasmuch as he is the descendent of the oldest son of this Louis Michelet. You yourself, Miss, however, belong to the same generation as my grand-children, the oldest of whom is also six years younger than yourself.

"After the information from your great-uncle, I at once attached the Genealogical Table of your American family, as far as it could be ascertained from it. You would place me under many obligations if, in accordance with your promise, you would send me a copy of the obituary notice of your great-uncle, as well as the names and births of all the American Michelets, for only then would I be able to perfect the so far only superficially prepared Genealogical Tree of your family.

"The photographs of your grandfather and father, I shall receive with many thanks, and that of myself shall not fail for you. I am exceedingly anxious to see whether the very decided family character of the Michelets has preserved itself in America as it has in the Michelet of Paris, whom I visited in 1849, and, as in a certain Norwegian, Adele Michelet, who introduced herself and her husband to us.

"These family features are so unmistakable that when, at a yearly festival of the French Huguenots here, my wife, Jenny, (a Swiss lady), saw the fur-dealer, Louis Michelet, without having known him previously, she turned to me and said, *"That is evidently a Michelet!"* In a remarkable manner is also yet familiar to my wife the saying of her great grandmother, *"They were perfect Michelets!"* My son, George, resembles me so strikingly in features and manners, that she is accustomed to say, *"This is a genuine Michelet!"* Eugene, the last, the apple of my eye, who followed his footsteps, has, alas, been taken away from me by a sudden death. What hopes had I built on him! How I reckoned on him once to continue my labors, as the oldest two have become physicians! He was a delicately framed, early matured boy, with beautiful large, animated blue eyes, with which he observed everything.

"With intelligent speech, he already realized the seriousness of life, and yet combined therewith a child-like cheerfulness and roguishness. With all my philosophy, I cannot realize nor get over the infinite loss.

"The visit of your mother's relative I await with pleasure, but would remark, in the meanwhile, that from July 7th to August 15th, we all expect to make a visit to the home of my wife. My visit to Hokendauqua I cannot, however, place in prospect before me, unless I should fare worse in Europe than is the case at present, for I soon will have to reckon eighty-two years. Your wishes for my health in coming years is heartily appreciated. With the request to be remembered to your relatives, though unknown to me, I remain your.

Most humble,
Michelet."

"Enclosed, herewith, you will receive the family Coat of Arms. So we brought it along from Metz, and so it is found in the "Book of Heraldry" in Vienna, as the Coat of Arms of the Family Michelet, in the free city of Metz, of the Germian Empire.

Mottoe: War, the Chase and Liberty.

"Upon a silver base there arises the pinnacle of a Fortress surrounded by a ditch. A deer, in its course, leaps over the same. The dome is adorned by a Cap of liberty. A tradition says that the Michelet family descends from the Spanish Miqueletos, hunters in the Pyrenees, who also served as soldiers in the armies of the Spanish Kings. Some of the members of the Berlin family and many of the Norwegian family have been officers or are as such yet."

The Michelet Family

Translation from Prof. Dr. C. L. Michelet's Autobiography or "Wahrheit aus Meinem Leben."

"I first saw the light of day in Berlin, on the 4th day of December, 1801, a child of the new century, and received in baptism the name of Charles Louis. Without wishing to inquire into the mysteries of astrology concerning my birth, at three o'clock on that winter's morning, I will only state that the day is consecrated to St. Barbara, the patroness of artillery-men, and that, in consequence of this coincidence, my life was destined to be a hard struggle with myself and others, for truth's sake. When the poet says,

"Man errs, as long as he strives,"

he expresses but an equivocal aphorism. For to strive is to seek; and he who seeks has not yet found. Therefore, he who strives after truth, does not yet possess it, and still dwells in error. I would preface this autobiography, with the axiom thus revised:

"Man struggles as long as he lives,"

and especially the philosopher — for the higher the object of the struggle, and with philosophers it is the highest, namely, truth, the hotter will the contest be — I might also add the motto:

"Miserrina est fortuna, quae inimico caret."

"According to the records, I belong on my father's as well as my mother's side to the French Calvinists, who, after the revocation of the Edict of Nantes, emigrated to Germany. My forefathers, and also the pioneers of this colony, were particularly bent upon contracting alliances for their children with members of their religious faith exclusively. Thus, if the purest French blood flows in my veins, my spiritual education, owing to circumstances, is thoroughly German. I once proposed to Victor Cousin, in a letter dated July 28, 1837, to become the mediator between the two nations, feeling myself almost providentially prepared for the undertaking, and as my French ancestors had been weavers of silk in their adopted home, so did I propose to introduce the web of German culture in my ancestral country. Cousin, however, in a most learned reply, dissuaded me from returning to Paris.

"I cannot fully decide whether, on my father's side, I am really of French extraction, the ancestral home of the Michelets being the old German Imperial City and Bishopric of Metz, but my mother's family, the Girards, were unquestionably from Dauphiné.

"That part of Lorraine in which Metz is situated, and which was dishonestly appropriated by Henri II in 1552, was called by the French *L'Allemagne,* more particularly, although it belonged to the Middle Kingdom situated between the two countries, and which had belonged to Lothair, together with the Roman Empire. If from this point of view we grant that these people, before the seizure by the French, were of German stock, we readily understand that after the entrance of the French conquerors, the original German population was by degrees obliged to adopt the French language and manners, particularly in the cities. There is every probability that my name was of pure German origin, *Michelchen* or Kleinmichel, and that later it was written Michel, with the addition of the French diminutive particle *let*, making it Michellet or Little Michel, as in the original. The name was later written with one *l*, but from the year 1444 to 1745, appears, with but one exception, with the double letter.

"When my son Paul, now a practising physician in Dresden, visited Metz, with the object of studying the family genealogy, he fortunately met a Protestant minister who had made a special study of the history of the families of Huguenot emigrants, and who was able to furnish us with the following interesting data, *i.e.*, that from Jehan Michelet, he who wrote his name with one *l*, down to myself, we are twelve generations, allowing 33 1/3 years to each. This data is perfectly reliable, as our informant had in his possession the complete records of the city of Metz and free access to the archives.

"Tradition points to a far more remote origin for the Michelets, than the middle of the 15th century — and to far more distant climes as its cradle, than the French province of Lorraine — namely, to Spain and the Pyrenees, far away in the dark ages, when a tribe of "Miquelettos," Mountain Robbers or Free-Booters, carried on their depredations on the frontier passes, whence they naturally penetrated into France. The very coat-of-arms of the Michelets would substantiate this myth, it represents on an argent field a fortress surrounded by a moat, a stag leaping over the parapet, and a liberty-cap crowning the helmet — War, the Chase and Liberty is therefore the motto of the Michelets, not to say the Miquelettos.

"Two missing branches of our genealogical tree have lately come to light, one coming from Norway from Captain Michelet of Drautheim, a direct descendant of Paul Michelet, an officer in the Danish army, who was present at the siege Drautheim in 1658. My other correspondent is Miss Minnie F. Mickley of Pennsylvania, a descendant of my great great-uncle, Jean Jacques Michelet, who emigrated to America in 1733 — with which the line is unbroken and complete."

The autobiography of Dr. Michelet is most interesting and learned through its seven hundred pages, and gives a complete picture of the life of a great German thinker and philosopher for nearly a century. Dr. Michelet is a hearty old man, retaining well his faculties, and still resides in the city of his birth. The volume closes with this characteristic epitaph, composed by the philosopher,. aPxd which is to be engraved on his stone,

"Sur la terre ici-bas il a trouvé le ciel;
Laiszy-lin saus la terre un repos éternal."

The following is the translation from the German of a paper found among the effects of the late Joseph J. Mickley, of Philadelphia, relating to the Mickley family:

INFORMATION

Relating to the Mickly Family, to its Origin and Further Extension from Authentic Sources, Vienna.

"The family 'Mickly' is an ancient French race of knightly and noble origin, that flourished already in the time of the Frank King Chlodwig, and was acknowledged as worthy consideration of importance.

"The first of this name (name father) is, according to the Chronicle of Gregor of Tours, a certain Dionysius Micheletus, who Originally came from Greece, where such a name conveys the meaning of illustrious,' of 'renown.' The Franconian Major-domo of the name Odeard brought such a Mickletus from Constantinople to Paris, where the latter became treasurer of King Chlodwig, and died A. D. 536. His descendants flourished yet till the times of the Emperor Carl the Great (Charlemagne), and called themselves Micklet, also Michelet, as the son, Edwin de Michelet, accompanied the aforesaid Emperor on his journeys to Spain, and in the combats in the Pyrenees and Basque Mountains, accomplished wonders of bravery.

"This Erwin had as consort an Isabella de Corsini, of Italian family, and dwelt upon the estate Chateau du Michelet, which lay in Provence. There, in extreme old age, he died, in the year 842, and left behind three sons, who were called Charles, Frederique and Denys de Michelet. The last two died as Abbots in French cloisters. Charles, however, had a Beatrice de Anjou, of royal blood, as wife, and dwelt in the castle of his race and name. He was Major-domo of the Franconian King Charles the Bold, and was so strong, that, in the neighborhood of Aries, he once cut in twain with one blow, a Norman knight, in full armor and coat of mail, so that the upper and lower parts of the body were completely separated. From his time on, one hears nothing again for a long time, and not until the time of Louis the Pious or Holy (probably St. Louis), one finds again news of this family. There was, namely, an Odarique de Michelet, who accompanied the said French King, A. D. 1249, upon his journeys to Egypt, and who lost his right hand during the siege of Damiette. He was happily cured, however, by the King's physician — called Harmanique de Salys. On his return, he married Eulalia Leontaras, who was the daughter of a Grecian prince, and who came from the Island of Cypress. From this time one finds this family living in peace upon their estate, but nothing specially noteworthy can one remark. Again, with the French King Francis I., is mention made of them. There was, namely, a Quentin De Michelet, the Colonel of a French Cuirassier Regiment, and who fought in the many battles of this

King in France, Italy and Germany with great honor. He had as wife Louison de Armaguacke, and left at his death, A. D. 1563, a son, who was called Bertrand de Michelet, He, also, was a distinguished soldier, and became artillery colonel. His usual residence he had at Dijon, where his artillery regiment was garrisoned. He found his death in the battle in the Netherlands, 1602. With his descendants one finds that they call themselves partly Mickly, partly Michelet. A scholar of this family, named Armand de Mickly, gave the inducement thereto, and he found out, collected and arranged the information regarding his family. He had his old and honorable coat-of-arms, the letters patent of his armoral bearings revived, made known, chartered and confirmed by King Louis XIV, and also by the German Emperor Leopold, and the ancient copy (deed) of such letters patent lays even yet in the archives of Paris and Vienna. His children, of whom he left five, lived yet at the end of the past century. But since the storm of the French Revolution, one finds no news of his family."

[Louis I of France was known as Louis the Pious, but Louis IV, commonly called St. Louis, must be the one meant here, as the first Louis lived about the sixth century, and made no journey to Egypt.

Seculi is probably intended for Säculum, a century, a cycle — and e has been used instead of ä. "So" is frequently used in the chronicle with the weight of "who" apparently — also once as "which."]

Prof. Dr. Michelet wrote the following letter after reading the "Information Relating to the Mickley Family:"

"Berlin, August 10th, 1889.

"Miss Minnie F. Mickley:

"*Dear Relative* — We were all very glad to have your dear father in our midst. Alas, the joy was a very brief one, for at the end of three days he left us again. Time was, indeed, very precious, and we made as much of it as we possibly could. At the end we were yet able to venture out, something which we could not do during your visit the previous year. We ended our joyful meeting with a visit to Tagel Castle, in order to see the burial place of the Humboldt family. In the midst of a woods, surrounded by the most luxuriant array of flowers, bedded around a high column, rest the departed members of the family, especially the two brothers, William, the minister and learned linguist, and Alexander, the great naturalist and universally acquainted traveller. The column is crowned with a statue of Hope, looking down upon the sleeping ones, executed by the Danish sculptor Thorwaldsen.

"Although both of my daughters, living in Charlottenberg, and their husbands were missing, having been on a sea voyage on the Baltic, nevertheless, I could count, with great satisfaction, at the supper on the shady summit of the park, nine Michelets, the number of the Muses, all of common birth, such as becomes the new world.

"As regards the family of nobility which Uncle Joseph has traced, there is no doubt but that such a family existed. Not only have I reliable information concerning such from Metz, but the Norwegian family Michelet has also discovered the same, and even sent me the coat-of-arms.

"You no doubt have again received the packet which you had sent me with your father. It gave me no new information, inasmuch as it was simply the original of the copy which you had sent me already. I am sorry that you cannot give me any further reliable data, since the authenticated papers were stolen from your uncle. I, consequently, find myself limited to my own researches, as the matter interests me very much. In fact, I have already begun the work, and have examined the Chronicles of Gregory, Bishop of Tours. I find, however, that he makes no mention of a Dionysius Mickletus, neither in the index nor in the text. Mickletus is to mean, in Greek, "renowned." But that should be Megakletos. Should I even make Meckletus out of this, the derivation would still not be beyond all my doubts. Heretofore, we have derived the name from the mountain hunters in the Pyrenees, the Miqueletos.

"I expect now to write to Vienna, in order to inquire into and get information concerning the coat-of-arms and the revival of nobility under Louis XIV and Emperor Leopold. It seems somewhat strange that the learned author of the narratives should already have called himself De Mickly in the seventeenth century, while your ancestor, Jean Jacques, is said to have assumed this name first, in the eighteenth century.

"Much of a mythical character is also connected with all, as for example, when a Michelet Knight is represented as slaying his enemy, in full armour, by cutting him from right to left, whereas Ariostos, "Raging Roland," is said to have done so by cutting from head to foot, so that the two parts of the body fell on either side of the war-horse. Still, that does not weaken the remaining part of the narrative.

"With many greetings to yours, I am.

Your,
Michelet."

The American Branch of the Mickley Family

In a collection of upwards of thirty thousand names of German, Swiss, Dutch, French, and other immigrants in Pennsylvania, from 1727-1776, by Prof. I. Daniel Rupp, under date of August 28th, 1733, are noted the names of persons arriving: Palatine, ship *Hope* of London, Dan Ried master, from Rotterdam, last from Cowes: Males, eighty-three, above sixteen; females, eighty-one; males and females, 225 under sixteen; in all 389. We find the names of Johan Jacob Mückli, also Johan David Deschler, Hans Jacob Schreiber, Hans Georg Kohler, Abraham Miller, and others, who settled in this region at the same time that John Jacob Mickley came. Members of these families afterward inter-married into the Mickley family.

Among the early settlers of Alsace or Elsace Township, Bucks County, were many French Reformed or Huguenots, also Swedes, who were Lutherans,

Germans and French, who located on the fertile lands of Wablink (encompassed by hills). Here an opening was made for other persecuted Huguenots. Amongst the prominent families in Oley were the Levans, Yoders, Schneiders, De la Plaines, De Lurcks, and others.

John Jacob Mickley came to this country a single man, and lived several years with Jacob Levan, in Oley, who was a relation of his. His daughter, Mrs. Bieber, told Joseph J. Mickley he was a "Veter" of her father's.

John Jacob Mickley bought land of Adam Deshler, a deed of which is in possession of the family from Adam Deshler to John Jacob Mickley, date December 14, 1761. A synopsis of the deed shows that the land was first deeded by William Penn to William and Margaret Lowther, 5,000 acres, date 23rd October, 1681. Amongst other deeds of John Jacob Mickley, first, second and third, are tracts of land known as "Oczakow," June 5th, 1789; an Indian name, meaning "at the Yellow Lands." The land is now known as "Mickleys," residence of Edwin Mickley; "Springfield," 1785; "Pond Brook," November 16, 1785; "Mount Pleasant," November 25, 1785. Other deeds of tracts of land from John Jacob Sr. to John Jacob Jr., date November 11th, 1801; June 22, 1804; June 3, 1820; two deeds dated December 19, 1826; August 4th, 1829.

Four hundred and fifty acres of the original tract of land, are now owned by descendants of John Jacob Mickley. It is to be hoped that more of the family will make Mickleys their future home; that village being entirely on the original tract.

In 1864, the undersigned, members of the Mickley family agreed to pay the sum set opposite their respective names, for the purpose of erecting a monument over the graves of John Jacob Mickley and his wife, who are buried in the Lehigh Valley, Lehigh County, Pa. The original stones were of slate, and the inscriptions were almost obliterated at the time. The following list was subscribed, but not being sufficient, Edwin Mickley added the required amount, and erected a neat tomb and inscription to the memory of John Jacob and his wife, Elizabeth Barbara Burkhalter, after the bodies were reinterred in Mickleys' Church Cemetery, Mickleys, Pa. The following is the list of subscribers, 1864: Abraham, William J., Hiram, Edwin, Annie B., Joseph J., Sallie M., William B., John, Ephram, Frank P., Henry, Peter, Abraham T., James, Daniel, Peter, Catherine, James W., Jacob and Henry J. Mickley; Mrs. Snively, Hannah Benkert, Mrs. Sarah Rau, Mrs. John Johnson, Henrietta Rau, Mary Jenkins, John Sheldon, Eliza Kuntz, Mrs. Christian Pretz, Joseph Swartz, Mrs. Samuel Glace, Mrs. Anna Sheldon, Mrs. V. W. Weaver.

A copy of the will of John Jacob Mickley No. 8, and all the papers relating to the settlement of his estate are carefully preserved.

Genealogy of the Mickley Family

In the archives of Metz, Germany, we find the following record:

1674-1675 — "Suzanne Mangeot was born June 26th, 1674, and was married 1697 to Louis Michelet, born December 17th, 1675, a merchant. He was blessed in his marriage with Suzanne Mangeot. He became a Protestant pastor at Zweibrücken, died February 27th, 1750.
The diary of Susanne Mangeot Michelet, now in possession of Prof. Dr. Charles L. Michelet of Berlin, Germany, states that "They remained at Zweibrücken until their son Jean Jacques was born and baptized."
1699 — Louis Michelet and his wife, Suzanne, born Mangeot, new converts to this Huguenot way. Converted to God, not acknowledging Roman Catholicism.
1715 — Louis Michelet, a widower, and his five children, Jean Jacques, Louis, Pierre, Barbé, Marie, new converts to the self-styled "Reformed Church."
— [*Extract from the Archives of Metz.*]
1697— John Jacob Mickley, or Jean Jacques Michelet, born ____, 1697; died August 18th, 1769.
1733— Eldest son of Louis Michelet and Suzanne Mangeot; came to America August 28th, 1733, and settled near what is now known as Mickleys, Lehigh County, and married Elizabeth Barbara Burkhalter, born ____, died August, 1769.

THE DESCENDANTS OF JOHN JACOB MICKLEY

One of the First Settlers of Lehigh (then Northampton) County.

FIRST GENERATION

Children of John Jacob — *Whitehall.* Married Elizabeth Barbara Burkhalter.

1 — John Jacob, born December 17th, 1737; died December 12th, 1808. Married Susanne Miller, born November 6th, 1743; died December 16th, 1807; Whitehall Township, Lehigh County, Pa.
He brought the Liberty Bell from Philadelphia to Allentown, arriving in Bethlehem, Pa., September 23d, 1777. He was a Revolutionary patriot, giving the use of his horses and wagons to the Continental Army, and helping in every way the cause of liberty. He was killed by a tree falling upon him, near his home, near Mickleys, Pa.
2 — John Martin, born March 3d, 1745; died March 11th, 1828. Married Catherine Steckel, born April 8th, 1749; died April 8th, 1830. Settled in Adams County, Pa., 1794.

He was a soldier in the Revolutionary War; was in the battle of Germantown.

3 — John Peter, born, 1752; died, 1828. Married Eva Keck, born ___, died ___.

He had a narrow escape from the Indians, October 8th, 1763. He was in the military service against the Indians, and in the War of the Revolution, during the whole time of its continuance, in the capacity of fifer. He was in the battle of Germantown. Settled in Bedminster Township, Bucks County, Pa., about the year 1784.

4 — Henry, born, 1754; died, October 8th, 1763.

Killed by Indians while chestnutting near Mickleys, Whitehall Township, Pa.

5 — Barbara, born, 1756; died October 8th, 1763.

Killed by Indians, Whitehall, Pa.

6 — Magdalena, born March 30th, 1745; died 1827. Married first, Peter Deshler, born March 18th, 1743; Irish Settlement, Northampton County, Pa. Married second, Michael Bierber (no heirs.)

7 — Susanne (?), born, ___; died, ___. Married Andrew Miller; (no heirs).

Note — For others of sixth generation in Europe see appendix. Louis of Berlin, 1720; Christian Frederick and Simon Themstrop, of Norway.

SECOND GENERATION

Children of John Jacob, 1 — Lehigh County, Pa.

8 — John Jacob, born April 13, 1766; died April 1, 1857. Married Eva Catherine Schrieber, born May 7, 1761; died September 16th, 1846.

He rode on the wagon bearing the Liberty Bell from Philadelphia to Allentown in 1777, and served as soldier in the Whiskey Rebellion of Pennsylvania in 1794. Died in the homestead at Mickleys, Pa.

9 — Christian, born, 1767; died, 1812. Married first, Elizabeth Deshler, born, 1773; died, 1840. She married second, Paul Balliet; born March 24, 1776; died, 1849; (no heirs of Balliet); Ballietsville. Pa., and Mickleys, Pa.

10 — Peter, born January 18th, 1772; died, 1861. Married Salome Biery, born, 1773; died 18—; Peter Mickley's place, near Hokendauqua. Pa.

11 — Henry, born July 10th, 1782; died May 27, 1827. Married Mary Magdalena Burkhalter, born, ___; died 1867; Mickleys, Pa., and Waterloo, N. Y.

12 — Joseph, born ___ (about) 1783; died, ___. Married Eliza Hartman, born, ___; died, ___; Franklin County, Pa.

13 — Daniel, born ___ (about) 1784; died, ___. Married (?) Tamer, a Quakeress supposed to have settled in Greensburg, Westmoreland County, Pa.

14 — Sarah, born November 27th, 1786; died January 25th, 1859. Married first, Henry Blumer, born, ___; died, ___. Married second, Jacob Stein, born October 17, 1778; died August 6, 1842.

15 — Anna, born, ___; died, ___. Married Joseph (?) Deshler, born, ___; died ___; Danville, Pa.
16 — Catherine M., born March 28th, 1764; died Janury 2d, 1835. Married John Balliet, born November 31st, 1761; died November 2d, 1837; Limestone ville, Montour County, Pa.
17 — Magdalen A. Married Woodring; Shamokin (?).

Children of John Martin, 2 — Adams County, Pa.

18 — John, born, 1769; died March, 1855. Married Margaret Biery, born, 1779; died February, 1852; Adams County, Pa.
19 — Peter, born, 1771; died February, 1860. Married Rebecca Dorothy Biery, born, 1775; died, 1857; Adams County, Pa.
20 — Margaret, born November, 9th, 1775; died July 6th, 1846. Married Jacob Saeger, born ___; died ___; Allentown, Pa.
21 — Catherine, born, 1778; died, 1875. Married Jacob Biesecker, Adams County, Pa.
22 — Susan, born, 1773; died, 1872. Married Frederick Biery, Allentown, Pa.
23 — Julia, born, 1776; died, 1864 (twin). Married John Piper, born, ___; died, ___; Huntington County, Pa.
24. — Daniel, born, 1776; died January, 1864 (twin). Married Salome Flohr, born, ___; died, ___; Adams County, Pa.
25 — Jacob, born, 1780; died, 1868. Married Barbara Hahn, born, ___; died, ___; Adams County, Pa.
26 — Maria Magdalena, born, 1778; died, ___. Married Jonas Hecker, born, 1771; died, 1842; Allentown, Pa.

Children of John Peter, 3 — Bucks County, Pa.

27 — Mary, born, ___; died, ___. Married George Snyder, Ohio.
28 — Catherine, born December, 1785; died April 20th, 1864. Married Jacob Beisher, born, ___; died, 1860; Bedminster Township, Bucks County, Pa.
29 — Maria, born, ___; died, ___. Married Andrew Snyder, born, ___; died, ___; Philadelphia, Pa.
30 — Susanna, born, 1788; died, 1878. Married George Henry Statzel; Philadelphia, Pa.
31 — Jacob, born, ___; died, ___. Died unmarried; Bedminster Bucks County, Pa.
32 — Peter, born February 20th, 1787; died December 23d, 1854. Married Mary Ott, born June 5th, 1796; died October 24th, 1869; Bedminster County, Pa. Served in the war of 1812.
33 — Hannah, born February 9th, 1795; died October 10th, 1884. Married Daniel Dieterly, born October 8th, 1796; died February 4th, 1863; Bedminster, Bucks County, Pa.

34 — Elizabeth, born November, 1791; died May 31st, 1871. Married Samuel Ott, born March 20th, 1791; died March 21st, 1857; Bedminster, Bucks County, Pa.

35 — Sarah, born April 5th, 1793; died February 1st, 1874. Married Samuel Kramer, born September, 1794; died December 5th, 1870, Rockhill, Bucks County, Pa.

36 — Barbara, born November 12th,, 1792; died July 17th, 1884. Married George Dieterly, born June 21st, 1788; died, 1861; Bedminster, Bucks County, Pa.

THIRD GENERATION

Children of John Jacob, 8 — Lehigh County, Pa.

37 — Mary Magdalexa, born, 17S9; died, , Married Daniel Moyer, born, ___; died, ___; Mercer County, Pa. (Major Mover.)

38 — Jacob, born March 27th, 1794; died June 2d, 1888. Married Anna Kern, born July 19th, 1795; died April 27th, 1879; Mickleys, Pa. Served in war of 1812-14.

39 — Sarah, born December 5th, 1790; died May 20th, 1817. Married John Schwartz, born, ___; died, ___; married second wife; Schwartz's, Northampton County, Pa.

40 — Anna, born March 4th, 1797; died September 28th, 1890. Married, first, John Youndt; second, Andrew Sheldon; Mickleys, Pa.

41 — Joseph, born March 24th, 1799; died February 15th, 1878. Married, first, Cordelia Hopfeldt; second, Diana Blumer; 903 Market Street, Philadelphia.

Children of Christian, 9 — Lehigh County, Pa.

42 — Peter, born July 17th, 1797; died February 20th, 1877. Married Anna Butz, born March 26th, 1800; died November 29th, 1880; Mickleys, Pa.

43 — Catherine, born, ___; died, ___. Married Daniel Seigfried; Lehigh County, Pa.

44 — Elizabeth, born, ___; died, ___. Married Peter Troxell, born, ___; died, ___; Allentown, Pa.

45 — Anna, born, ___; died, ___. Married Wasser, Lehigh County, Pa.

46 — Magdalen A, born, ___; died, ___. Married Charles Burkhalter; Lower Milford, Lehigh County, Pa.

47 — Sarah, born, ___; died, ___. Married Hass; Mercer County Pa.

Children of Peter, 10 — Lehigh County, Pa.

48 — Mary Magdalena, born April 8th, 1792; died, 1889. Married Daniel Snyder; Bloomsburg Pa.

49 — Catherine, born March, 1795; died, ___. Married Daniel Burkhalter, born, ___; died, ___; Clinton County, Indiana.
50 — John, born April, 1796; died, 1796, near Hokendauqua.
51 — Salome, born September, 1798; died, 1867. Married John Troxell; Mechanicsville, Lehigh County, Pa.
52 — Hannah, born October, 1800; died, 1881. Married, first, Joseph Kern; second, George Ludwig; Allentown, Pa.
53 — Joseph, born January, 1802; died, 1832, Married Catherine Miller, born, ___; died, ___; Trexlertown, Lehigh County, Pa.
54 — Charles, born October, 1802; died, 1878. Married Henrietta Fegley, born, died,; Mechanicsville, Lehigh County, Pa.
55 — Elizabeth, born October, 1805; died, 1845. Married George Fahler, born, ___; died,; Allentown, Pa.
56 — Christina, born, 1808; died, 1885. Married John Peter Byle, born, ___; died, ___; Seigfried's Bridge, Pa.
57 — Susanna, born March, 1811; living in 1892. Married Thomas Moyer; Tamaqua, Pa.
58 — Esther, born September, 1815; died, ___. Married Stephen Troxell; Clinton County, Indiana.

Children of Henry, 11 — Lehigh County, Pa.

59 — Magdalena, born, 1804; died June 21st, 1875. Married Joseph Seigfried, born, ___; died September 26th, 1879; Waterloo, N. Y.
60 — Anna, born, 1806; died December 14th, 1882. Married John. Deshler, born, ___; died, ___; Waterloo, N. Y.
61 — Edward B., born, 1808; died, 1885. Married Catherine Troxell; Waterloo, N. Y.
62 — Deborah, born, 1811; died December 10th, 1869. Married David Fegley, born, ___; died January 14th, 1862; Waterloo, N. Y.
63 — William B., born June 30th, 1813. Married Sarah Alleman, born May 12th, 1818; Waterloo, N. Y.
64 — Charles, born, 1815; died, 1878. Married Margaret Frantz; Waverly, Iowa.
65 — Stephen, born, 1818. Married Sarah Frantz; Le Mars, Iowa.
66 — Thomas, born April 5th, 1820. Married Margaret Miller, born, ___; died, ___; Waverly, Iowa.
67 — James, born, 1826; died, ___. Unmarried; Allentown, Pa. Served in Mexican War, 1847.

Children of Joseph, 13 — Lehigh County, Pa.

68 — Mary Anna, born, ___; died, ___. Married George Bell, born, ___; died, ___; Adams County.
69 — Sarah, born, ___; died, ___. Married John Beisecker; Delphi, Indiana.

70 — Catherine, born December 11th, 1820; died September 1st, 1S73. Married Martin L. Miller, born December 29th, 1818; died December 22d, 1891, near Castletown, Adams County, Pa.

71 — Eliza, born, ___; died, ___. Married John Barkdsell, born, ___; died, ___; Illinois.

72 — Anna, born, ___; died, ___. Married Benjamin Lutz, born, ___; died, ___; Indiana.

Children of John, 18 — Adams County, Pa.

73 — John, born, 1796; died, 1882. Married Harriet Kantzleman, born, ___; died, ___; Fairfield, Pa.

74 — Elizabeth, born, 1797; died, ___. Married George Diehl, born, ___; died, ___; New Oxford, Adams County, Pa.

75 — Sarah, born, 1799; died, ___. Married George Plank; Gettysburg, Pa.

76 — Daniel, born, 1801; died, 1867. Married Eliza Walter, born, ___; died, ___; Fairfield, Pa.

77 — Hester, born, 1804; died, ___. Married George Plank, (second wife); Gettysburg, Pa.

78 — Margaret, born, 1807; died, ___. Married Christian Musseliman, born, ___; died, ___; Fairfield, Pa.

79 — David, born, 1816. Unmarried; Ortanna, Pa.

80 — Martin, born, 1822. Married Anna Crook; Fairfield, Pa.

81 — Harriet, born, 1828; died, 1861. Married Levi Pitzer; Ortanna, Pa.

Children of Peter, 19 — Adams County, Pa.

82 — Daniel, born December 8th, 1795; living in 1892. Married Elizabeth Settle, born January 13th, 1796; died March 19th, 1873.
Served in the war of 1812. Company A, Riflemen, at the bombardment of Fort McHenry, Waynesboro, Adams County, Penna.

83 — Peter, born, 1797; living in 1892. Married (first) Rebecca Pitzer, (second) Anna Heretor, died, ___; Cashtown, Pa.

84 — Henry, born, 1799; died, 1890. Married (first) Rebecca Reynolds, (second) Elizabeth Rebert, (third) Elizabeth Settle, living; Seven Stars, Pa.

85 — James, born, ___; died, ___. Married Harriet Hershy, born, ___; died, ___; Adams County, Pa.

86 — Abraham, born, ___; died, ___. Unmarried; Martin Mickley Homestead, Adams County, Pa.

87 — Rebecca, born, ___; died, ___. Married Henry Bushy; Wyattsville. Pa.

88 — Hester, born, 1804; died, 1887, Married Nicholas Bushy, born, ___; died, ___. Married second, Conrad Lower, born, ___; Hornstown, Pa.

89 — Margaret, born, ___; died, ___, Married Peter Hake, born, ___; died, ___; York County, Pa.

90 — Susan, born, ___; died, ___. Married Israel Arendt, Arendtsville, Pa.

91 — Sarah, born, ___; died, ___. Married Jacob Heretor; Gettysburg, Pa.

Children of Daniel, 25 — Adams County, Pa.

92 — Elizabeth, born, 1798; died, 1889. Married Henry Walter; Virginia.
93 — Sarah, born, 1802; living in 1892 (twin). Married Abraham Plank; near Gettysburg, Pa.
94 — Daniel, born, 1802; died, 1876 (twin). Married Catherine Shull, born, ___; Cashtown, Pa.
95 — Peter, born, 1804; died, 1862. Married Sarah Myers; Florhs, Pa.
96 — Jacob, born November 15th, 1806; died December 9th, 1884. Married Mary Knause; Florhs, Pa.
97 — John, born July 24th, 1808; died March 15th, 1872. Married Elizabeth Boyer; Voltaire, York County, Pa.
98 — Rebecca, born, 1810; died, 1889. Married John Hinman, Lancaster, Pa.
99 — Maria, born, 1812; living in 1S92. Married Kenry Comfort, born, ___; died, ___; Gettysburg, Pa.
100 — Joseph, born April 18th, 1814; died December 5th, 1883. Married (first) Harriet Policy, born, ___; died, ___; (second) Rebecca Biesecker, born, ___; died, ___; Fairfield, Pa.
101 — Abraham, born, 1814. Married Lydia Myers, born, ___; died, ___; New Salem, Ohio.
102 — Kate, born, 1817. Married Peter Comfort, born, ___; died, ___; Gettysburg, Pa.
103 — Charles, born, 1815. Married Jane Green; Orrglen, Pa.
104 — Eli, born, 1822; died, 1860. Married Elizabeth Shull; Frederick, Md.
105 — Augustus, born, 1825. Married Elizabeth Stover, born, ___; Cashtown, Pa.

Children of Jacob, 25 — Adams County.

106 — Susanna, born, 1807; died, ___. Unmarried, near Cashtown, Penna.
107 — Mary Magdalena, born 1808; died November 24th, 1891. Married Daniel Hantzleman; Cashtown, Pa.
108 — Hannah, born, 1811; died, ___. Unmarried; Cashtown, Pa.
109 — Rebecca, born, 1808; died, ___. Married Samuel Bercaw. near Cashtown, Pa.
110 — Sarah, born, 1822; died, ___. Married Samuel Pettis; near Cashtown, Pa.
111 — Elizabeth, born, 1818; died, ___. Married John Trostle; near Cashtown, Pa.
112 — Charlotte, born, 1815; died, ___. Married John Donalson; near Cashtown, Pa.
113 — Ephraim, born, 1827; died, 1878. Unmarried; Adams County, Pa.
114 — Jereivhah, born, 1829; died, 1875. Unmarried; Adams County, Pa.

115 — George, born, 1824; died, 1824; Cashtown, Pa.
116 — Julia, born, 1813; died, ___. Married (first) White, (second) Miller, (third) Wilson; Gettysburg, Pa.
117 — Daniel, born, 1816; died, 1867. Married Martha Bucher; near Cashtown, Pa.

Children of Peter, 32 — Bucks County, Pa.

118 — Aaron, born, 1817; died, 1818; Bedminster, Pa.
119 — Levi Ott, born August 7th, 1819; died, 1862. Married Lucy Ann Worman; Pipersville, Bucks County, Pa.
120 — Hannah, born, 1821. Married Jacob Fackenthall, born, ___; died, ___; Doylestown, Pa.
121 — Josiah, born, 1824. Married Elizabeth Dieterley; Bedminster, Pa.
122 — Amanda, born August 10th, 1827. Married William White, born, ___; died, ___; Doylestown, Pa.
123 — Peter Ott, born, 1832. Married Lydia Ann Eckert; Margaret, Kansas.

FOURTH GENERATION

Children of Jacob, 38 — Mickleys, Pa.

124 — Mary, born, 1824. Married Valentine Weaver, born,;lMacungie, Pa.
125 — Rebecca, born, 1825; died November 16th, 1S91. Married Samuel Thomas, born, ___; Catasauqua, Pa.
126 — Ephraim, born August 18th, 1826; died October 9th, 1887. Married Elizabeth A. Deshler, born, ___; died, ___; (no heirs.)
127 — James W., born September 27th, 1828; died October 16th, 1880. Married Annie Leisnering Cooper; Catasauqua, Pa. Served during the Civil War, 1861-65.
128 — Edwin, born April 20th, 1830. Married Matilda E. Fogel, born October 6th, 1834; homestead, Mickleys, Pa.
First Lieutenant, Company B, Thirty-eighth Regiment, Pennsylvania Volunteer Militia; Com.-Gens. Zeigel and Warren.
129 — Catherine A., born, 1832; Allentown, Pa.
130 — Eliza, born, 1834. Married Rev. David Kuntz; Lutheran pastor; Nazareth, Pa.
131 — William Jacob, born September 18th, 1836; died May 16th, 1891. Married Lucy Keck, born, ___; Alburtis, Pa.
132 — Jane, born, 1838. Married Enoch Phillips; Pulaski City, Va.
133 — Anna Lovina, born, September 12th 1818; died April 14th. 1823; Mickleys, Pa.
134 — Francisca, born December 19th, 1824; died March 1st, 1839; Mickleys, Pa.

Children of Joseph, 41 — Philadelphia, Pa.

135 — Henry Joseph, born July 10th, 1828. Married Mary Ann Majilton, born, ___; died, ___; 1329 South Fifteenth street, Philadelphia, Pa.
136 — Josephine C. A., born September 25th, 1830; died August 9th, 1887. Married John J. Johnson, born, ___; Thirty-eighth and Sansom streets, Philadelphia, Pa.
137 — Hannah C, born July 4th, 1835. Married George Benkert, born, ___; died, 1885; London, England.
138 — John Jacob, born November 23d, 1836; died December 6th, 1892. Married Emma Lois Luther; (no heirs); Visalia, California.
139 — Sarah Julia, born July 2d, 1839. Married William C. Wilson, born, ___; Laramie City, Wyoming.
140 — Joseph Phillip, born May 26th, 1842; Mickleys, Pa.
Past Assistant Engineer of the United States Navy. Served in Federal Navy during the Civil War, 1861-65.

Children of Peter, 42 — Mickleys, Pa.

141 — Eliza A., born, 1818; died, 1818; Mickleys, Pa.
142 — Thomas, born, 1819; died, 1842. Unmarried; Mickleys, Pa.
143 — Abraham, born November 2d, 1826. Married Maria Erdman, born, ___; Mickleys, Pa.
144 — Franklin Peter, born March 1st, 1832. Married Sarah Butz, born, ___; Ballietsville, Pa.
145 — Caroline Susanna, born August 12th, 1836. Married Francis Levan, born, ___; died, ___; Coplay, Pa.
146 — Maria A. E., born, 1839; died, 1842; Mickleys, Pa.
147 — Alfred Thomas, born, 1842. Married Sarah Smith, born, ___; (no heirs); Mickleys, Pa.

Children of Joseph, 53 — Lehigh County, Pa.

148 — David, born September 1st, 1826. Married Maria Frantz, born, ___; died, ___; Ironton, Pa.
149 — Charles, born January 27th, 1832; died October 22d, 1862. Married Eliza Heimbach, born, ___; died, ___; Allentown, Pa.
Captain, Company G, Forty-seventh Regiment, killed in action, October 22d, 1862; Franklin, South Carolina,
150 — Amanda, born December, 1825. Married Henry Schadt, born, ___; Ruchsville, Pa.
151 — Hannah, born January 27th, 1821. Married Ludwig Wolf, born, ___; Allentown, Pa.
152— Catherine, born 1832. Married John Zeigler; Mechanicsville. Pa.

Children of Charles, 56 — Trexlertown, Pa.

153 — Anna C, born August, 1830. Married John Sieger, born, ___ died, 1890; Seigersville, Pa.
154 — Isabella, born, 1828; died, 1830; Trexlertown, Pa.
155 — Matthias C., born November 1st, 1832; died March 3d, 1888. Married Augusta Dorr, 1873; St. Cloud, Minn.
156 — Henry Louis, bora, 1834. Married ___; Hamburg, Pa.
157 — Mary Anna, born, 1837. Married Moses Guth, born, ___ Guths, Pa.

Children of Edward B., 61 — Waterloo, N. Y.

158 — Franklin, born, 1833. Married Anna Callorn, born, ___; Waterloo, N. Y.
159 — Henry Clay, born, 1836. Married Mary Mountain; Mansfield, Ohio. Fiftieth Regiment, Engineers, Civil War 1861-65, New York.
160 — Erastus, born, 1848. Married Margaret Clement, born, ___;. Seneca Falls, N. Y.
161 — Delancy, born, 1860; Senaca Falls, N. Y.
162 — Catherine B., born, ___; Waterloo, N. Y.
163 — Edson L., born, 1859; died, 1889; Waterloo, N. Y.
164 — Edwin, born, 1839; died, 1839; Waterloo, N. Y.
165 — Adeline, born, 1842; Waterloo, N. Y.
166 — Frances E., born, 1856. Married William A. Mosher, Seneca Falls, N. Y.

Children of William B., 62 — Waterloo, N. Y.

167 — Bayard Taylor, born October 1st, 1850; died December 17th, 1855; Waterloo, N. Y.
168 — Dewitt, born June 14th, 1859; Waterloo, N. Y.
169 — Susan J., born January 23d, 1858; Waterloo, N. Y.
170 — Elsie Lee, born February 12th, 1852. Married Oliver Perry Loveridge; Waterloo, N. Y.
171 — Alice R,, born November 12th, 1S55. Married Hon. J. Erastus Richardson; Waterloo, N. Y.
172 — Georgianna, born Nov. 17th, 1S57. Married Isaac Westbrook; Fayette County, N. Y.
173 — Clara Belle, born October 4th, 1861; Waterloo, N. Y.
174 — Helena, born November 26th, 1864; Waterloo, N. Y.

Child of Charles, 64 — Iowa.

175 — Joseph, died at five years of age.

Children of Stephen, 65 — Iowa.

176 — Henry, born, ___. Unmarried; LeMars, Iowa.
Served in the New York Third Light Artillery, Civil War, 1861-64.

177 — Hudson, born November 25th, 1846. Married Mary Frink, born, ___; Auburn, N. Y.
Served in New York Third Light Artillery during the Civil War, 1861-64.
178 — Emma, born November 26th, 1849. Married Joseph Comine, born, ___; Janesville, Iowa.
179 — Cora, born, ___; LeMars, Iowa.

Children of Thomas, 66 — Iowa.

180 — Stephen, born November 28th, 1841. Married Sarah Miller, born, ___; Buffalo, N. Y.
181 — William, born September 22d, 1845. Married Kate Hatfield; 262½ Union street, Jersey City, N. J.
182 — Francis, born February 13th, 1S51. Married A. Van Nordstrand; Waverly, Iowa.
184 — Jane, born May 1st, 1850. Married Homer Healy; Janesville, Iowa.

Children of John, 73 — Adams County, Pa.

185 — Mary M. J., born, 1858. Married Samuel Bomgardner; Fairfield, Pa.
186 — Harriet Rebecca, born, 1860. Married Latimer Myers; Fairfield, Pa.
1S7 — Sarah, born, 1861. Married William Gulp; near Fairfield, Pa.
188 — John, born, 1864. Married C. C. Scott, born, ___; Philadelphia, Pa.
189 — Emma F. S., born, 1868. Married John Trostle; Fairfield, Pa.

Children of Daniel, 76 — Fairfield, Pa.

190 — Daniel born, ___; Fairfield.
191 — Abraham, born, ___; Fairfield.
192 — William, born, ___; Fairfield.
193 — Elizabeth, born, ___; Fairfield.

Children of Martin, 79 — Fairfield, Pa.

194 — Annie, born, ___. Married George Gordon, born, ___; Franklin County, Pa.
195 — Ida, born, ___. Married Jacob Cleek; Adams County, Pa.
196 — Robert, born, ___; Waynesboro, Pa.
197 — Margaret, born, ___; Waynesboro, Pa.
198 — Blanch, born, ___; Waynesboro, Pa.

Children of Daniel, 82 — Waynesboro, Pa.

199 — Catherine, born February 20th, 1821. Married Jonas Bell, born, ___; Waynesboro, Pa.
200 — Mary, born February 21st, 1825. Married Daniel Bell; Waynesboro, Pa.

201 — Sarah, born October 10th, 1824; died September 30th, 1890. Married George Summers; Waynesboro, Pa.
202 — Susan, born March 26th, 1826. Married Daniel Good; Waynesboro, Pa.
203 — Peter, born January 23d, 1828; died September 4th, 1854. Married Margaret Gilbert, born, ___.
Killed by lightning near Green Castle, Pa.
204 — Henry, born October 10th, 1829. Married Sarah Summers; Franklin, County, Pa.
205 — Elizabeth, born April 25th, 1831; died, 1863. Married George Stephy; Waynesboro, Pa.
206 — Daniel, born June 18th, 1833. Unmarried; Waynesboro, Pa.
207 — Abraham, born September 26th, 1834; died December 24th, 1890. Married Sarah Stephy; Waynesboro, Pa.
208 — Mary Ann, born June 30th, 1836; died, 1859. Unmarried; Waynesboro, Pa.
209 — John, born March 1st, 1838; died, 1863; Waynesboro, Pa. Killed in battle near Charlestown, Va., Seventeenth Pennsylvania Cavalry.
210 — Simon, born October 9th, 1841. Married ___; Waynesboro, Pa.

Children of Peter, 83, — Cashtown, Pa.

211 — Esther, born, 1822. Married George Hagerman, born, Cashtown, Pa.
212 — Dorothy Rebecca, born, 1825; died, ___. Married Joseph Rebert; Cashtown, Pa.
213 — Magdalena, born, 1827; died, ___. Married James Rebert; Cashtown, Pa.

Children of Henry, 84 — Seven Stars, Pa.

214 — James, born, 1828. Married Mary Hershy; near Gettysburg, Penna.
Captain Company C, 182d Regiment, Pennsylvania Volunteers. Served throughout the war, 1861-65.
215 — Harriet, born, 1830. Married George Hershy; Gettysburg, Pa.

Children of Daniel, 94 — Cashtown, Pa.

216 — Jacob, born October 11th, 1S24. Married Eliza Pitzer, born, ___; McKnightstown, Pa.
217 — Israel, born June 22d, 1S28; died February 23d, 1862. Married Elizabeth Rife, Cashtown, Pa.

Children of Peter, 95 — Florhs, Pa.

218 — Jeremiah Marion (Rev.), born, 1836. Married Emily C. Fraine.
Chaplain of Company —, Regiment, 1861-65, in General Crook's command, against the Apache Indians. Pastor of the German Reformed Church, McKnightstown, Pa.

219 — Hiram, born, 1837; died, 1869. Married Charlotte Mundorff; Gettysburg, Pa. Soldier in Civil War, 1861-65.
220 — Melinda, born, 1839. Married Thomas Cover; Gettysburg, Pa.

Children of Jacob, 96 — Florhs, Pa.

221 — Eli, born, 1843; died, 1863. Married Mary Rook; Funkstown, Franklin County, Pa. Soldier in Civil War, 1861-65.
222 — William, born, ___. Married (first) Sarah Fritz; (second) Miss Lily; Columbus. Ohio. Served in Civil War. Six months in Libby Prison.
223 — James, born, ___. Married Elizabeth Singley, born, ___; Fairfield, Pa.
224— Hannah Mary, born, ___. Married Jessie Metz; Fairfield, Pa.
225 — Salome, born, ___; Fairfield, Pa.
226 — Peter, born, ___; died, 1862; Fairfield, Pa. Killed in battle, Civil War, 1861-65.
227 — Jane, born, ___. Married George Plershy, born, ___; Cashtown, Pa.
228— Emma, born, ___. Married George Shellman; Cashtown, Pa.
229 — Rebecca, born, ___. Married Grant Funt; Cashtown, Pa.
230— Minnie, born, ___; died, ___; Waynesboro, Pa.
231 — Lillie, born, ___; Waynesboro, Pa.
232 — Bertie, born, ___: Waynesboro, Pa.
233 — Ella, born, ___; Waynesboro, Pa.
234 — Harriet, born, ___. Married Joseph Bennett; Waynesboro, Pa.
235 — Margaret, born, ___. Married Charles Pitzer; Waynesboro. Pa.
236 — Annie, born, ___; Waynesboro, Pa.
237 — Matilda, born, ___. Married George Little; Waynesboro, Pa.
238 — George, born, ___; Waynesboro, Pa.

Children of John, 97— Voltaire, York County, Pa.

239 — Lavina, born November 3d, 1836. Married Joseph Reeser; Hale, York County, Pa.
240 — Adam, born December 27th, 1838. Married Hannah Laird; Voltaire, York County, Pa.
241 — Sarah, born February 1st, 1841; died November 4th, 1843; York County, Pa.
242 — Edward, born March 1st, 1843. Married Catherine Doll, York County, Pa.
243 — Solomon, born February 27th, 1845. Married Elizabeth Baker; Roanoke, Huntington County, Indiana.
244 — Anna M., born March 27th, 1847; died March 1st, 1854; York County, Pa.
245 — Aaron, born April 25th, 1847. Married (second) Rose Gladfelter; Baltimore, Md.
246 — Charlotte, born February 27th, 1852. Married Peter Salterham; Mt. Royal, York County, Pa.

247 — Lucinda, born May 26th, 1854. Married Peter Baublitz, Strinestown. Pa.

248 — Rebecca, born June 24th, 1857. Married Peter Braum, York, Pa.

249 — John, born April 1st, 1864; died July 3d, 1865; York, Pa.

Children of Joseph, 100 — Fairfield, Pa.

250 — Anna S., born July 27th 1845; died February 27th, 1846; Fairfield, Pa.

251 — Urias a., born September 2d, 1839. Married Margaret Biesecker, born, ___; Denver, Colorado. Served in Civil War. Six months in Libby Prison.

252 — Elias Franklin, born March 24th, 1849. Married Mary Herbert; Perth, Sumner County, Kansas.

253 — Amos Wesley, born October 11th, 1850; died October 11th, 1867; Fairfield, Pa.

254 — Sarah Salome, born June 22d, 1852. Married Ezra Fuss, Kansas.

255 — Charles, born, ___. Married Miss Forney; Belle Plain, Kansas.

256 — Henry, born, ___; died, ___. Unmarried; Fairfield, Pa.

257 — Naomi Elizabeth, born July 5th, 1854; died October 7, 1877. Married Robert Ogden; Fairfield, Pa.

258 — David Augustus, born May 29th, 1856. Married Sarah Mussleman, born, ___; died, ___; Fairfield, Pa.

259 — Rebecca Jane, born February 13th, 1858. Married John D. Brown; Fairfield, Pa.

260 — Charles Edward, born July 10th, 1860; Fairfield, Pa.

261 — Margaret A., born August 10th, 1862. Married John A. Donalson, Fairfield, Pa.

262 — Maria Sherman, born January 8th, 1865. Married Daniel Stoops; Fairfield, Pa.

263 — Anna M. C., born June 13th, 1867. Married John Wetzel; Fairfield, Pa.

264 — Joseph H., born April 24th, 1875; died April 9th, 1888; Fairfield, Pa.

Children of Abraham, 101 — New Salem, O.

Nine children; all died in childhood.

Children of Charles, 103 — Orrglen, Pa.

265 — Samuel, born, 1843; died, 1847; Orrglen, Pa.

266 — Lemuel, born February 1st, 1849. Married (first) Margaret A. Grimers; (second) Ida F. Ford; Syracuse, N. Y.

267 — Americus Green, born January 20th, 1850. Married Henrietta Mickley; Cashtown, Pa.

268 — Avilla, born January 6th, 1847. Married Rev. David W. Wolff, born, ___; died, ___; Orrglen, Pa.

Child of Eli, 104 — Frederick City, Md.

269 — Sarah, born, ___; Frederick City, Md.

Children of Augustus, 105 — Cashtown, Pa.

270 — Emmaline Alice, born, 1845; died, 1862; Cashtown, Pa.
271 — John Augustus, born, 1848. Unmarried; Cashtown, Pa.
272 — Elliot Parker, born, 1849. Married Millicent Gorden; near Cashtown, Pa.
273 — Mervin O., born, 1854. Married Catherine Adams; near Cashtown, Pa.
274 — Sarah, born, 1850. Married William Cover; McKnightstown, Pa.
275 — Charlotte, born, 1856. Married Charles Thorn, born, ___; died, ___; Gettysburg, Pa.
276 — Mary E., born, 1862; Cashtown, Pa.
277 — Sherry Frederick, born, 1849; died, 1862; Cashtown, Pa.

Child of Daniel, 117 — Cashtown, Pa.

278 — John Alfred, born, ___. Married Clara Blocher; Cashtown, Pa.

Children of Levi Ott, 118 — Bucks County, Pa.

279 — Lucinda, born January 16th, 1817; died October 27th, 1872; Bedminster, Pa.
280 — Pearson W., born November 25th, 1848. Married Mary Everhart; No. 210 Green Street, Philadelphia.
281 — Mary E., born July 10th, 1851. Married William Sheetz, Philadelphia, Pa.
282 — Helena, born May 14th, 1854, Philadelphia, Pa.

Children of Josiah, 121 — Bedminster, Pa.

283 — Reed, born March 29th, 1857; died October, 1877; Bedminster, Pa.
284 — Euphemia, born May 9th, 1864; died March 7th, 1886. Married William S. Nicholas; Bedminster, Pa.

Children of Peter Ott, 123 — Margaret, Kansas.

285 — Ida E., born December 22d, 1861. Married Edwin Saunders; La Joya, New Mexico.
286 — Harvey, born July 27th, 1863; died January 26th, 1867; Margaret, Kansas.
287 — Lycurgus, born May 25th, 1865; died January 12th, 1867; Margaret, Kansas.
288 — Granville, born July 4th, 1867; died July 11th, 1871; Margaret, Kansas.

289 — Mary, born April 17th, 1869; Margaret, Kansas.
290 — Eleanora, born April 1st, 1871. Married John M. Saunders, La Joya, New Mexico.
291 — Cora, born September 27th, 1875; Margaret, Kansas.
292 — John Jacob, born March 8th, 1876; Margaret, Lincoln County, Kansas.

FIFTH GENERATION

Children of James W., 120 — Catasauqua, Pa.

293 — Edith Righter, born, 1863; died, 1869; Catasauqua, Pa.
294 — Harry Thomas, born, 1865; died, 1865; Catasauqua, Pa.
295 — Edgar Cooper, born, 1866; died, 1869; Catasauqua, Pa.
296 — Anna Edith, born, 1869; died, 1871; Catasauqua, Pa.
297 — Carrie Euphemia, born, 1870; died, 1876; Catasauqua, Pa.
298 — John Cooper, born, 1872; died, 1872; Catasauqua, Pa.
299 — Bessie Cooper, born, 1874; died, 1877; Catasauqua, Pa.
300 — James William, born, 1877; died, 1877; Catasauqua, Pa.
301 — Frederick Wilhelm, Catasauqua, Pa.
302 — Mabel Cooper, Catasauqua, Pa.
303 — Ralph Cooper, Catasauqua, Pa.

Children of Edwin, 128 — Mickleys, Pa.

304 — Anna Ophelia Desdemona, Mickleys, Pa.
305 — Lillie Ellen Eva. Married Dr. Henry Martyn Chance, Wayne, Pa.
306 — Minnie Fogel, Mickleys, Pa.
307 — John Jacob, Mickleys, Pa.

Children of William, 131 — Albnrtis, Pa.

308 — Stella, Alburtis, Pa.
309 — Elma Carrie, born November 16th, 1869; died May 12th, 1878; Alburtis, Pa.

Children of Henry J., 136 — Philadelphia, Pa.

310 — Albert Joseph. Married ___; Newport News, Va.
311 — Henry Jacob, Philadelphia, Pa.
312 — Edgar Majilton, Philadelphia, Pa.

Children of Abraham, 142 — Mickleys, Pa.

313 — Alice M. A. Married M. Newhard; near Allentown, Pa.
314 — Oscar Franklin. Married Jemima Schadt; Ruchsville, Pa.
315 — Preston T. Erdman. Married Susan Long; Mickleys, Pa.

316 — Amanda M., born, 1858; died, 1889. Married Frank J. Henninger; near Ironton, Pa.
317 — Joseph Benjamin. Married Laura Kohler; Coplay, Pa.
318 — Ida Hannah. Married Oliver B, F. Breinig; near Mickleys.
319 — Franklin Peter, born September, 1864; died, 1878; Mickleys.
320 — Sarah Jane, born, 1866; died, 1872; Mickleys, Pa.
321 — Edwin Abraham, born, 1868; died, 1872; Mickleys, Pa.
322 — William John, born, 1871; died, 1872; Mickleys, Pa.

Children of Franklin Peter, 143 — Ballietsville, Pa.

323 — Ella C. Married Walter Bieber; Kutztown, Pa.
324 — Annie S. Married James B. Albright; Washington, D. C.
325 — Laura. Married Alvin Hauck; Easton, Pa.
326 — Howard, M. D. Married Margaret Koch; Ballietsville, Pa.
327 — Charles Franklin; Allentown, Pa.

Children of David, 147 — Ironton, Pa.

328 — Albert Joseph. Married Emma Brader; Easton, Pa.
329 — Frances Peter, born May 5th, 1857; died, 1857; Ironton, Pa.
330 — Heinrich Jacob; Brainard, Minn.
331 — Amanda Caroline. Married Frank Lucas; Catasauqua, Pa.
332 — Urias David, born, 1855; died, 1855; Ironton, Pa.
333 — Mary Ann E. Married John Biery; Ironton, Pa.
334 — Crisse Drusilla, born, 1859; died, 1864; Ironton, Pa.
335 — Ellen Jane. Married Mr. Kugler; Easton, Pa.

Children of Charles, 148 — Allentown, Pa.

336 — Sarah Ann. Married James B. Hammersly, South Sixth Street; Allentown, Pa.
337 — Winfield Scott, born June, 1848; died, 1871; Allentown, Pa.
338 — William Deshler. Allentown, Pa. Captain Company ___, Pennsylvania Militia.
339 — Charles Henry. Married Sarah Bohler; Allentown, Pa.
340 — Thomas Franklin; Allentown, Pa.
341 — Caroline. Married Nicholas Paul; Allentown, Pa.
342 — John Heimbach, born, 1859; died, 1866; Allentown, Pa.

Children of H. Lewis, 156 — Hamburg, Pa.

343 — Lewis. Married Barbara Burkhalter; Hamburg, Pa.
344 — Henrietta. Married ___, Nyce; Hamburg, Pa.

Child of Franklin, 158 — Waterloo, N. Y.

345 — Francis Wright, Lincoln, Nebraska.

Children of Henry Clay, 159 — Mansfield, Ohio.

346 — Franklin B., Seneca Falls, N. Y.
347 — Frederick M., Cleveland, Ohio.
348 — Irene E. Married Rufus A. Kern, Mansfield, Ohio.
349 — Edward B., Mansfield, Ohio.
350 — Clarence H., Mansfield, Ohio.

Child of Erastus, 160 — Seneca Falls, N. Y.

351 — Annie E., Seneca Falls, N. Y.

Child of Stephen D., 161 — Seneca Falls, N. Y.

352 — Henry L., Seneca Falls, N. Y.

Children of Hudson, 177 — Auburn, N. Y.

353 — Maud Aileen. Married D. Edward Poulein; Washington, D. C.
354 — Eva, Auburn, N. Y.
355 — Le Roy, Auburn, N. Y.
356 — Jessie Fay, Auburn, N. Y.

Children of Stephen, 180 — Buffalo, N. Y.

Children of William H., 181 — Jersey City, N. J.

357 — Lida, Jersey City, N. J.
358 — Lena M., Jersey City, N. J.
359 — Herbert W., Jersey City, N. J.
360 — Zillah L., Jersey City, N. J.

Child of Peter, 203 — Greencastle, Pa.

361 — Clara, Greencastle, Pa.

Children of Henry, 204 — Franklin County, Pa.

362 — Daniel, Harrisburg, Pa.
Cumberland Valley Railroad.
363 — Lavina. Married Thomas Smith; Waynesboro, Pa.

Children of Abraham, 207 — Waynesboro, Pa.

364 — J. Harvey, (Rev.) Scottsdale, Pa. Pastor of Scottsdale Reformed Church.

365 — Daniel, Waynesboro, Pa.
366 — Nora, Waynesboro, Pa.
367 — Emma, Waynesboro, Pa.

Children of Simon 210 — Waynesboro, Pa.

368 — John, Philadelphia, Pa.
369 — Mary, Waynesboro, Pa.
370 — Marshall, Waynesboro, Pa.
371 — Adelaide, Waynesboro, Pa.
372 — Grace, Waynesboro, Pa.
373 — Edna, Waynesboro, Pa.
374 — Annie, Waynesboro, Pa.

Children of James, 214 — Near Gettysburg, Pa.

375 — Savilla. Married Jacob Sheely; Cashtown, Pa.
376 — Lucy Ann. Married Daniel H. Deardorff; Cashtown, Pa.
377 — Henrietta. Married Americus G. Mickley; Cashtown, Pa.
378 — Marietta. Married Dill Henry; Cashtown, Pa.

Children of Jacob, 216 — McKnightstown, Pa.

379 — Frank. Married Sarah Lohr; New Salem, Ohio.
380 — Morgan. Married Mary Erb; McKnightstown, Pa.
381 — Catherine. Married John Hartman; Mumasburg, Pa.
382 — Annie, born March 11th 1857; died March 17th, 1892. Married Robert Myers, Table Rock, Pa.
383 — Virginia. Married Harvey Plank; McKnightstown, Pa.
384 — Lydia. Married Abram Warren; McKnightstown, Pa.

Children of Israel, 217 — Cashtown, Pa.

385 — David. Married Mary Jane Winter; Cashtown, Pa.
386 — Isaac. Married Ida Trostle; Cashtown, Pa.
387 — Clara. Married William M. Rebert; Cashtown, Pa.

Children of Rev. J. Marion, 218 — McKnightstown, Pa.

388— Edgar Lee. Married Hannah F. Kam; McKnightstown, Pa.
389— Lillie Alice. Married Dr. Ephraim Shellenberger; Carlisle, Penna.

Children of Hiram, 219 — Gettysburg, Pa.

390 — Anna Belle. Married Rev. ___ Reichard.
391 — Sallie Myers, Gettysburg, Pa.
392 — Mary Lincoln, born March 15th 1866; died, 1867; Gettysburg, Penna.

Children of Eli, 221 — Franklin County, Pa.

393 — Emma, born, ___; died, ___; Funkstown, Pa.
394 — George, Funkstown, Pa.
395 — Alice, Funkstown, Pa.

Children of William, 222 — Columbus, Ohio.

396 — Harry, Columbus, Ohio.
397 — Cora, Columbus, Ohio.
398 — Daniel, Columbus, Ohio.
399 — Franklin Monroe, Columbus, Ohio.
400 — Marietta, Columbus, Ohio.

Children of James, 223 — Fairfield, Pa.

401 — George Oliver, Fairfield, Pa.
402 — Daisy Bell, Fairfield, Pa.
403 — Effie May, Fairfield, Pa.
404 — Margaret Kate, Fairfield, Pa.
405 — Jane, Fairfield, Pa.
406 — James Roy, Fairfield, Pa.

Children of Adam, 239 — Voltaire, York County, Pa.

407 — Mary Elizabeth. Married John Lowers; Voltaire, Pa.
408 — Emma Jane. Married B. F. Hinkle; Voltaire, Pa.
409 — Annie Maria. Married H. G. Miller; Voltaire, Pa.
410 — John. Married Kate Aldinger; Voltaire, Pa.
411 — Charles, Voltaire, Pa.
412 — Adam, Voltaire, Pa.
413 — Silas, Voltaire, Pa.

Children of Edward, 240 — York, Pa.

414 — Avilla, born July 15th, 1862; died, 1872; York, Pa.
415 — Sarah Jane, born May 15th, 1775; died, 1872; York, Pa.
416 — Laura. Married Paul W. Stine; York, Pa.
417 — Savilla, York, Pa.
418 — Israel Rush, York, Pa.

Children of Soloman, 241 — Roanoke, Ind.

419 — Sarah Ellen. Married Jacob Dubbs, Roanoke, Ind.
420 — John A., born August 31st, 1866; died, 1866; Roanoke, Ind.
421 — Jacob C. Married Cora A. Zent; Roanoke, Ind.
422 — Joseph E. Married Claudia Hubley; Roanoke, Ind.

423 — Thomas F., Roanoke, Ind.
424 — Anis R., born June 1st, 1876; died, 1877; Roanoke, Ind.

Children of Aaron, 242 — Baltimore, Md.

425 — Louise Jane. Married Fred Althen; York County, Pa.
426 — Harry, York County, Pa.
427 — Cora, York County, Pa.
428 — Harvey, York County, Pa.
429 — Carrie, York County, Pa.
430 — Daisy, York County, Pa.
431 — Alberta, Baltimore, Md.
432 — Charles, Baltimore, Md.
433 — Anna, Baltimore, Md.

Children of Urias, 250 — Denver, Colo.

434 — Melvin, Denver, Col.
435 — Grant, Denver, Col.

Children of Elias, 251 — Perth, Kansas.

436 — Wesley Alexander, Perth, Sumner County, Kan.
437 — Elmer Elsworth, Perth, Kan.
438 — John Joseph, Perth, Kan.
439 — Frank Ferdinand, Perth, Kan.

Children of David A., 257 — Fairfield, Pa.

440 — Cora May, Seven Stars, Pa.
441 — Mary Alberta, Seven Stars, Pa.
442 — Bertha Bell, Seven Stars, Pa.
443 — Eva Grace, Seven Stars, Pa.
444 — Fannie Delta, Seven Stars, Pa.

Children of Lemuel, 265, Adams County, Pa.

445 — Golden Mildred, Syracuse, N. Y.
446 — Roland Earle, Syracuse, N. Y.

Children of Americus G., 266 — Cashtown, Pa.

447 — Clarence, Cashtown, Pa.
448 — Arthur, Cashtown, Pa.
449 — Clarice, Cashtown, Pa.
450 — Sallie, Cashtown, Pa.
451 — Stella, Cashtown, Pa.

Child of Elliot P., 271 — Cashtown, Pa.

452 — Mitchell Stover, Cashtown, Pa.

Children of Mervin O., 272 — Cashtown, Pa.

453 — Anna May, near Cashtown, Pa.
454 — Cora E., Cashtown, Pa.
455 — Bertha K., Cashtown, Pa.
456 — Robert Eugene, Cashtown, Pa.
457 — Millie Irene, Cashtown, Pa.
458 — Mary Edith, Cashtown, Pa.
459 — Roy Augustus, Cashtown, Pa.
460 — John Oscar, Cashtown, Pa.

Children of John A., 277 — Cashtown, Pa.

461 — Maud, Cashtown, Pa.
462 — Guy, Cashtown, Pa.
463 — Nora, Cashtown, Pa.

Children of Pearson N., 279 — Philadelphia, Pa.

464— Charles Levi, born March 13th, 1877; died, 1879; Philadelphia, Penna.
465 — Samuel Augustus, born February 13th, 1879; died, 1884; Philadelphia, Pa.
466 — Annie E., born, 1885; died, 1886; Philadelphia, Pa.
467 — Katie E., born, 1S87; died, 1887; Philadelphia, Pa.
468 — Pearson, born, 1890; died, 1890; Philadelphia, Pa.
469 — Thomas Edward, Philadelphia, Pa.
470 — Elizabeth Grace, Philadelphia, Pa.

SIXTH GENERATION

Children of Oscar F., 314 — Riichsville, Pa.

471 — Eva H., Ruchsville, Pa.
472 — Thomas B., Ruchsville, Pa.
473 — Edwin A., Ruchsville, Pa.
474 — Ida May, Ruchsville, Pa.
475 — Helen Margaret, Ruchsville, Pa.
476 — L. Annie M., Ruchsville, Pa.
477 — Daniel R., Ruchsville, Pa.

Children of Preston T., 315 — Mickleys, Pa.

478— Ella M., Mickleys, Pa.
479 — Marcus W., Mickleys, Pa.
480 — Howard Levan, Mickleys, Pa.

Child of Joseph B., 317 — Coplay, Pa.

481 — Irene, Coplay, Pa.

Children of Albert Joseph, 328 — Easton, Pa.

482 — James Garfield, Easton, Pa.
483 — Irwin, Easton, Pa.
484 — Edward, Easton, Pa.
485 — Mary E., Easton, Pa.

Child of Franklin B., 346 — Seneca Falls, N. Y.

486— Harold, Seneca Falls, N. Y.

Children of Franklin, 379 — New Salem, O.

487 — Henry William, New Salem, O.
488 — Samuel Jacob, New Salem, O.
489 — Calvin, New Salem, O.

Children of Morgan, 380 — McKnightstown, Pa.

490 — Virginia, McKnightstown, Pa.
491 — Daisy, McKnightstown, Pa.

Children of David, 384 — Cashtown, Pa.

492 — Blanch Elizabeth, Cashtown, Pa.
493 — Maud Catherine, Cashtown, Pa.

Children of Isaac, 385 — Cashtown, Pa.

494 — Edna, Cashtown, Pa.
495 — Elizabeth Grace, Cashtown, Pa.

Child of Edgar, 387 — McKnightstown, Pa.

496— William Lee, McKnightstown, Pa.

Child of John, 411 — York, Pa.

497 — Gertrude, York, Pa.

Additional Names too late for Classification:

FIFTH GENERATION

Children of C. Matthias, 154 — St. Cloud, Minn.

498 — Edward G., born June 18th, 1872; died, July 16th, 1875; St. Cloud, Minn.
499 — Lewis J., St. Cloud, Minn.
500 — Clara G., St. Cloud, Minn.
501 — Arthur P. J., St. Cloud, Minn.
502 — Matthias F., St. Cloud, Minn.

GENERAL SUMMARY

The following is a summary of the number of descendants of John Jacob, in the different generations, as given in the preceding catalogue:

First Generation.................................... 7 names.
Second "... 28 names.
Third ".. 87 names.
Fourth ".. 169 names.
Fifth ".. 185 names.
Sixth ".. 27 names.

Total..503

War Record

The following is a list of the descendants of John Jacob Mickley in the different generations, who served in the wars of the United States, as patriots, officers and privates.

WAR OF THE REVOLUTION

John Jacob (No. 1). A patriot. He conveyed the State House bell (the old Liberty Bell) from Philadelphia to Allentown, and gave the use of his horses and wagons to the Continental Army.

John Martin (No. 2). A soldier. Was in the battle of Germantown, October 4th, 1777.

John Peter (No. 3). A fifer. Was in the battle of Germantown, October 4th, 1777. He served throughout the whole of the Revolutionary War.

WHISKEY REBELLION OF 1794. (PENNSYLVANIA.)

John Jacob (No. 8). A soldier. Went with State militia to the western part of the State in June, 1794. Washington disbanded the army.

WAR OF 1812

Peter (No. 32). A soldier.
Jacob (No. 38). A soldier. Served in Captain Ruhe's Company, Marcus Hook. He was also commissioned Second Lieutenant of a troop of cavalry within the bounds of the Sixty-eighth Regiment of the Militia of the Commonwealth of Pennsylvania, Second Brigade, Seventh Division of the Militia, composed of Counties of Northampton, Pike and Lehigh; by Governor Joseph Hiester, August 20th, 1821, until August 3d, 1828. Daniel (No. 82). A soldier. Company A Riflemen, at bombardment of Fort McHenry, September 13, 1814.

MEXICAN WAR, 1846-47.

James (No. 67). A soldier.

THE CIVIL WAR, 1861-65.

James W. (No. 127). Union Army. Company D, Eighth Regiment, Pennsylvania Volunteer Militia, 1862.
Edwin (No. 128). Union Army. First Lieutenant, Company B, Thirty-eighth Regiment, Pennsylvania Volunteer Militia, 1863.
Charles (No. 149). Union Army. Captain Company G, Forty-seventh Regiment, Pennsylvania Volunteers. Killed in battle of Pocotaligo bridge, near Franklin, South Carolina, 1S62.
Joseph Philip (No. 140). United States Navy. Appointed Acting Third Assistant Engineer (cadet), March 28th, 1864, by Gideon Welles, Secretary of the United States Navy, under President Abraham Lincoln.
During the war he did duty on the U. S. S. "Coeur-de-Lion," Potomac Flotilla, on the Potomac, Rappahannock, James, York and other rivers, with base of supplies at Belle Plain, during the battle of the Wilderness. July 14th, 1865, U. S. S. "Muscoota," Gulf Squadron. On U. S. S. "Yucca" for purpose of wrecking U. S. S. "Jacinto" during the yellow fever epidemic on board ship. There were only two officers on duty for three days — Messrs. Mickley and Durand. October 13th, 1866, U. S. S. "Resaca," from Portsmouth, N. H., on a trip around South America via Strait of Magellan to join the North Pacific Squadron, and thence from San Francisco to Russian America (now Alaska) to freeze out yellow fever, and assist in receiving the country from Russia, which was purchased March 20th, 1871.
Commissioned Second Assistant Engineer (master), by President U. S. Grant, December 30th, 1871. Ordered to U. S. S. Monitor "Terror" Gulf Squad-

ron. January 25th, 1873, ordered North in charge of prisoners sentenced by General Court Martial, and delivered them to the Commandant of the Navy Yard, New York. April 8, 1873, U. S. S. "Lackawanna" Asiatic Squadron; joined her at Shanghai, China. On December 24th, U. S. S. "Ashuelot" visited Japan, China, Cochin China, Singapore and Siam, 1,300 miles up the Yang-Tse River, China, being the first American vessel to visit the port of Ichang, 350 miles beyond the treaty port of Hankow. February 24th, 1874, commissioned Assistant Engineer (junior lieutenant) by President U. S. Grant.

April 29th, 1877, Iron clad "Wyandotte" Navy Yard, Washington, D. C., ordered with the Monitors "Passaic" and "Montauk," to protect the Treasury Department during the railroad riots of 1877. He passed through epidemics of yellow fever, cholera, smallpox on four cruises and escaped from the fatal disease in each instance. Commissioned as Passed Assistant Engineer (lieutenant) by President R. B. Hayes.

October 18th, 1878, ordered to U. S. S. "Ticonderoga" on a special cruise around the world in the interest of commerce. Renewed treaties with Zanzibar, Arabia and Birmah, and attempted to open Corea. Commodore Shufeldt, returning to Corea for that purpose. September 20th, 18S4, U. S. S. "Powhatan" on special coast service. November 6th, 1886, U. S. S. "Yantic" with Home Squadron. January 7th, 1891, on Dynamite Cruiser "Vesuvius." On March 20th, 1891, ordered to the Dispatch vessel "Fern" on special duty.

Henry Clay (No. 151). Union Army. Fiftieth Regiment, Engineers, New York Volunteers, 1861-65.

Henry (No. 176). Union Army. Third Light Artillery, New York, 1861-65.

Hudson (No. 177). Union Army. New York Third Artillery Volunteers, 1861-65.

James (No. 214.) Union Army. Captain Company C, 182d Regiment, Pennsylvania Volunteers, 1861-65.

J. Marion (No. 218). Chaplain and staff officer. Under special orders and in different commands. In the Army of the Potomac (except the battle of Gettysburg); was at that time with a detachment in North Carolina. His last service was in connection with General Sheridan's expedition through the South. He helped to man the regular forts along the Rio Grande River. Stationed at Fort Brown, Texas; lost two horses in battle during the war. In 1873-74 was under General Crook against the Apache Indians, in lower California and Arizona.

Hiram (No. 219). Union Army. Two Hundred and Ninth Pennsylvania Regiment of Infantry; joined Ninth Army Corps. He participated in the retaking of "Fort Hell" before Petersburg, Va., in the last year of the war, 1861-65.

John (No. 209). Union Army. Seventeenth Pennsylvania Cavalry. Killed in battle near Charlestown, Va.

Eli (No, 221). Union Army. Soldier, 1861-&5.

William (No. 222). Union Army. Soldier. Six months in Libby Prison.

Peter (No. 226). Union Army. Killed before having been in battle.

STATE MILITIA

William Deshler (No. 338). Captain Company B, Pennsylvania Militia. Served duty at Homestead, Pa., August, 1892.

European Genealogy

FIRST GENERATION

LA FAMILLE MICHELET DE METZ

(D'prés des documents authentiques.)

Les Enfants de Jehan Michelet — Le Masson, 1444.

I — Jean ___ Michelet, le boucher investé de l'order de Saint-Michel par Louis XI, 1471, Seigneur de Beauval, Departement de la Somme.
2 — Antoine Jacques Michelet. Seigneur d'Interville, President au Parlement de Rouen, 1596, portant les mêmes armòries que les Seigneurs de Beauval.
3 — Anne Michelet de Beauval, épousa en 1615, Charles de la Ville Auffrai, Baron de Paynel-Mercy.
4 — Claude, hoste à la Rochelle daus la rue Princerie á Metz, 1482.
5 — Etienne, le Bolangier, 1542.
6 — Claude, rescripvain, 1565.
7 — Jacques on Jacquemin, escripvain, 1576; clerc, 1579; receveur, 1587; commis du trésorier du Roy, 1593, morte, 1610; premiere femme, Suzanne Joly, morte, 15S4, seconde femme Suzanne Wiriot.
8 — La Soeur Marguérite, femme de Claude Estienne, 1572.

SECOND GENERATION

Les Enfants de Jacques, No. 7 — De sa premiere femme Suzanne Joly.

9 — Jacques, baptized 14th October, 1576; ancien, morte, 30th of October, 1651.
10 — Susanne, baptized 18th of January, 1579, 6p. Michel Persode de Savoie.
11 — Pierre, baptized 20th of Juin, 1582; pasteur, morte, 6th of Mars, 1632. De son épousa Marie, fille de Daniel Lenoir, Seigneur de Meis, morte le 19th of Juin, 1626, él ent un fils.
12 — Paul, baptized 16th of Décember, 1584, diacre, fermier des moulins de la ville, épousa Anne, fille de Josué Pillon, receveur des deniers de la bullette. De sa seconde femme, Suzanne Wiriot.

13 — Daniel, baptized 20th of September, 1592; épousa Marie fille de Daniel Collin, pratician du palais.
14 — Samuel, baptized 22d of Juillet, 1598.
15 — Esther, baptized 23d of Mars, 1603, morte venue de David de la Cloche, 8th of Avril, 1661.

THIRD GENERATION

Le Fils de Pierre, No. 11.

16 — Gédéon, Marchand, Seigneur.

Les Enfants de Paul, No. 12.

17 — Paul, baptized the 5th of September, 1617. Émigrés en Norvége, 1644; Lieutenant, 1644; Major, 1658; Starb. 1659.
18 — Jacques, baptized the 7th Avril, 1619. Émigrés en Norvége, 1644.

Les Enfants de Daniel, No. 13.

19 — Daniel, baptized the 18th of Décember, 1615; morte, 21st of Juin, 1659, or firve; épousa Judith fille de David de la Cloche, or firve.
20 — Esther, baptized the 20th of January, 1619; morte fille, 12th of Mai, 1684.
21 — Jacques, baptized the 29th of Décember, 1623; morte, 8th of October, 1685, teinturier, diacre.
22 — Suzanne, baptized the gth of Mai, 1627; morte, Févr. 20th, 1668.

FOURTH GENERATION

Le Fils de Gédéon, No, 16.

23 — Pierre, baptized the 21st of Décember, 1657; morte, 1699. Colonel des milices, émigré à Berlin, 1685.

Les Enfants de Daniel, No. 19.

24 — Daniel, baptized the 21st of November; 1649; morte, 29th of November, 1670.
25 — Suzanne, née the 24th of Décember, 1653; morte, 1711. Refugee avec son Mari Quien a Berlin.

Les Enfants de Jacques, No. 21.

26 — Anne, née the 19th of Févr., 1619; morte, 1681. Veuve Dubois.
27 — Pierre, 1652. Mercier, diacre.
28 — Jacques, baptized the 16th of Févr., 1661. Teinturier.

29 — Louis, née the 17th of December 1675. Marchand, aprés pasteur a Zweebrücken, épousa Suzanne Mangeot á Zweebrücken.

FIFTH GENERATION

La Fille de Pierre.

30 — Judith, morte, 1702, á Berlin.

La Fille de Pierre, No. 23.

31 — Anne, née the 28th of January, 1682, épousa de David Girard.

Les Enfants de Louis, No. 24.

32 — Jean Jacques, née 1697; morte Aout. 18th, 1769, d Zweébrücken, émigré, 1733, de Zweébrücken en Amérique. Épousa Elizabeth Barbara Burkhalter, morte, August, 1769. Whitehall, Pa.
33 — Jeanne, née the 15th of November, 1699, a quitté Metz, 1708, avec la Comtesse de Nassau.
34 — Barbe, 16th of November, 1702.
35 — Marie, 11th of December, 1703.
  Refugee de Metz, á Berlin, ou elle épousa Pierre Perrin.
36 — Louis, 8th of December, 1705: morte, 1766. Émigré de Metz á Berlin 1720.
37 — Pierre, 21st of Décember, 1710.
  Les enfants de Louis, No. 24 — Jean, Louis, Pierre, Barbe, Marie passent á Metz, en 1715, an protestantisme, comme leurs parents l'avient fait en 1699.

SIXTH GENERATION

FAMILLE MICHELET DE BERLIN

Louis Michelet, No. 36.

Arrivé á Berlin avec David Girard le neveu de son père, pour être apprenti dans la Société pour la fabrication des Soireries Girard, Michelet et Companie, y entra plus tard comme associé. La raison de commerce est restée pendant trois générations dans la famille:

Les Enfants de Louis, No. 36.

38 — Louis, née 11th of Juin, 1736; morte, 17th of Juillet, 1800.
39 — Marie Francotse, née 15th of Août., 1738; morte, 10th Fèvre., 1796. Épousa Baudouin.

40 — Pierre, née 24th October, 1741; morte, 9th Fevre., 1787. Officer de hussards sous Frederic II.
41 — Robert David, née 226. Juin, 1744; morte, 20th November, 1802. Associé de la fabrique de soirie.

SEVENTH GENERATION

Les Enfants de Louis, No. 38.

42 — Madelaine, née 24th Mai, 1764; morte, i-8th Janvier, 1839.
43 — Marie Susanne, née isth Mai, 1765; morte, 13th October, 1780.
44 — Louis, née 1st Mars, 1775; morte, 6th Fevre., 1841. Épousa Girard.
45 — Henrietta, née 17th Mars, 1776; morte, 18th Fevre, 1844. Veuve de Ed. Jordan.

Les Enfants de Robert David, No. 41.

46 — Louis, née 5th October, 1773; morte, 23d September, 1808.
47 — Henri, née 1778; morte, 11th Avr., 1803. Jurisconsulte.
48 — Augusté, née 1780; morte, 24th Juin, 1858. Rentier.
49 — Edoward, née 14th September, 1788. Capitaine pendant la guerre de 1813-15.
50 — Manon.
51 — Jenny. Épousa Mr. Bock.
52 — Pauline.

EIGHTH GENERATION

Les Enfants de Louis, No. 44.

53 — Charles Louis, née 4th Décember, 1801. Professeur de Philosophie à l'Université. Premiere épousa, Marie Scholz, née 18th December, 1813; morte, Mai 14th, 1864. Deuxiéme épousa, Jenny Vallon née 3d Julliet, 1839; morte, 1886. No, 16 Burgraffen Strasse, Berlin, Germany.
54 — Carline, née 4th Janvr, 1803. Épousa Poppe.
55 — Victoire, née 18th Mai, 1813; morte, 18th Mars, 1872. Épousa Dünnwald.

Les Enfants de Louis, No. 46.

56 — Emilie, née 28th Décember, 1800. Épousa le graveur Thieme.
57 — Anne, née 1st October, 1802. Épousa Platz.
58 — Elizabeth, née 21st Décember, 1803. Épousa le Confiseur d'Heureuse.
59 — Louis, née 3d Fevr., 1805 morte, environ 1876. Pelletier.

NINTH GENERATION

Les Enfants de Charles Louis, No. 53.

60 — Paul, né 18th Décembre, 1835. Medicin á Dresden.
61 — Jenny, née 3d Novembre, 1850. Épousa le Dr. Dünwald, fils.
62 — Charles, né 24th Avr., 1854. Épousa Anna Michelet veuve. Medecin á Berlin.
63 — Louisa, née 14th Octobre, 1868. épousa Adolph Gertz.
64 — George, né 14th Octobre, 1870; Berlin.
65 — Helens, née 16th September, 1873.
66 — Eugene, né 25th Mai, 1878; morte, 16th Mai, 1883.

Les Enfants de Louis, No. 58.

67 — Louis, né 24th Juin, 1833; morte, 24th Septembre, 1879. Courtier, agent de change.
68 — Paul, né 26th Octobre, 1835. Pelletier.
69 — Richard, né 28th Mars, 1810. Banquier.
70 — Marianne, née 5th Dccembre, 1841. Épousa le conseiller municipal Haalk.

ILLS ONT TOUS FAMILLE.

TENTH GENERATION

Les Enfants de Paul, No. 59.

71 — Paul, né 10th Juin, 1866. Dresden
72 — Marie, née 7th Févr., 1870. Dresden.
73 — Ilse, née 13th Avril, 1872. Dresden.

FOURTH GENERATION

NORWEGISCHER ZWEIG DER FAMILLIE

Paul Michelet, No. 17.

74 — Johann, 1650; bis 9th März, 1716. Hauptmann.
75 — Christian Frederick, 5th März, 1697; bis 30th Janun., 1769. Oberst Lieutenant.

FIFTH GENERATION

Children of Christian, No. 74.

76 — Jorgen, 1st Juni, 1742; bis 26th February, 1818. General.

77 — Militar.
78 — Militar.
79 — Milltar.
80 — Géislicher.
81 — Johann Wilhelm Géislicher, 13th November, 1753; bis 27th December, 1805.

SIXTH GENERATION

Children of Johann W., No. 79.

82 — Christian Frederick, 7th December, 1792; bis 13th Mai, 1874. General in Fredericks Stadt.
83 — Simon Themstrop, 6th December, 1793; bis 9th November, 1879. Officier, dann General-Einnehmer.
84 — Kaufmann.
85 — Land-Eigenthümer.
86 — Johann Wilhelm, geboren 2d November, 1805. Hauptmann, dann Steuer-Beamter.

SEVENTH GENERATION

Children of Christian, No. 80.

87 — Rechts-gelehrter.
88 — Rechts-gelehrter.
89 — George V., Ramel-Michelet. Oberst Lieutenant.
90 — Adelheid, Ebemann, Saxlund, Ryfoged in Friedrich's Halle. Zwei Enkel des Generals sind Krieger.

Child of Simon Themstrup, No. 81.

91 — Hauptmann, in Drontheim.

GENERAL SUMMARY

The following is a summary of the number of descendants of Jean Michelet of Metz, in the different generations as given in the preceding catalogue:

First Generation	8	names.
Second "	7	"
Third "	6	"
Fourth "	7	"
Fifth "	8	"
Sixth "	4	"
Seventh "	11	"
Eighth "	6	"
Ninth "	11	"
Tenth "	3	"
	71	"

NORWEGIAN BRANCH.

Fourth Generation	2	names.
Fifth "	6	"
Sixth "	5	"
Seventh "	5	"
Norwegein branch	18	"
German "	73	"
	91	"
American "	503	"
	594	"

Joseph J. Mickley - A Biographical Sketch by His Friend J. Bunting

As published in Lippincott's Magazine of July, 1885, and now reproduced by kind permission of J. B. Lippincott & Co.

Joseph J. Mickley.

Not many years ago there were several substantial old houses standing on the north side of Market street, east of Tenth, in the city of Philadelphia. These structures, which then wore an air of respectable old age, have been in recent years either totally destroyed or so extensively altered that the serene atmosphere of antiquated gentility no longer lingers about their busy exteriors.

On a morning in April, 1869, the present writer had occasion to call at one of these buildings — No. 927. Several broad and weather-stained marble steps led up to an old-fashioned doorway, where the modern bell-pull and the antique brass knocker contended for recognition. Alike rusty as these were, it became a problem as to which would best secure communication with the interior.

The Late Joseph J. Mickley, of Philadelphia, PA.

While the matter still seemed indefinite, it was set at rest by the advice of an obliging street urchin, who volunteered his information with appropriate brevity and directness:

"Try the door. If it's loose. Daddy Mickley's home, sure. If it's locked, 'taint no use of knockin', for he's out."

Thus instructed, I tried the door. It happened to be "loose," and ushered me into a long dark entry, at the farther end of which a wide flight of heavy oak stairs led to the upper rooms in the rear of the building. Among these rooms, one of the first to be reached was evidently a workshop; and here was encountered the only living being as yet visible in the spacious old mansion. Upon entering, I was met by a dignified and placid old gentleman, whose appearance was very much in keeping with the house in which he dwelt. He was quite evidently of the old school, and his pleasant voice gave me an old-school welcome. A fine broad forehead rested above a pair of the most kindly eyes that can be imagined, and belonged to a splendidly-shaped head, which was totally bald, save for a slight fringe of white hairs about either temple. The mouth was, in its expression, even more prepossessing than the eyes, and the whole bearing of the old gentleman — who had evidently reached his threescore and ten, but who, as was equally apparent, carried the warmth and vigor of youth still with him — was calculated to please and impress the least observant visitor.

The late Joseph J. Mickley comprised qualities at once more attractive and more unusual than are often met with in one person. He was distinguished throughout the world, during more than a generation, for the diligence and success of his numismatic researches, and his collection of rare coins was for a long time the most valuable in this country. As a collector of scarce books and autographs he was hardly less noted or less successful. But in Philadelphia he was most of all admired for his delightful social qualities and his extensive information on a surprising variety of topics. During forty years his house was a rendezvous for a numerous group of specialists — not alone in his own favorite pursuits, which, indeed, were both many and diverse, but in any and every department of art or learning. Coin-hunters, autograph dealers, historical students, philosophers, musical instrument-makers, noted performers, and performers of less note, all the way down to "scratch-clubs," were his constant visitors for years. It is probable that no private house in Philadelphia has entertained a greater number of intellectually distinguished people than the old mansion just referred to, where Mickley resided from 1842 to 1869. Musical celebrities from every country hastened to make his acquaintance, and such was the magnetism of his personality that acquaintances thus formed seem never to have been lost sight of by either host or guest. During his European tour, which lasted from 1869 to 1872, the then venerable traveler was continually meeting friends among persons who had called upon him at various times, dating back in one case as long before as 1820. They always appeared to have known beforehand of his coming, and he always remembered them and the circumstances under which he had first met them.

The social reunions at Mickley's were informal to the last degree, and the accommodations correspondingly primitive. They usually took place in his workshop. Crazy stools or empty piano boxes generally served for seats. The surrounding furniture comprised barrels. cases and chests, filled to overflowing with the host's ever-increasing antiquarian treasures. If a quartette were assembled — and many times the musical party was enlarged to a quintette or a septette — an adjournment was necessary to a room less crowded, but equally sparse of conventional furniture.

Mr. Mickley was always happy to join in these impromptu musical assemblies, when occasion offered, although performing music was one of the few things which he never succeeded in doing well. He invariably played the viola on these occasions — perhaps, as Schindler hints about Beethoven, because indifferent playing on the viola is not so noticeable as on other instruments. As was to have been expected from so pronounced an antiquarian, he had small sympathy for modern music. He even rebelled against the gentle innovations of Mendelssohn, contending, not without an approach to accurate judgment, that Haydn and Mozart had completely covered the field of chamber music. While in the midst of numerous and always congenial pursuits during his long life, quartette pla3dng remained a favorite pastime of very many days in very many years.

Mr. Mickley's intellect was so many-sided and so evenly balanced that it is difficult to name his predominant bias. It is very nearly safe, however, to say that this was his historic faculty. In the writings, still chiefly unprinted, which were left behind him, he was at once the most minute and the most compact of historians. Emerson never condensed his rare thoughts into smaller compass^ not even in his "English Traits," than Mr. Mickley has condensed his facts and observations. There is a small pamphlet extant, the manuscript of which was read by him in 1863, on the occasion of the centennial anniversary of a noted Indian massacre in Northampton County, Pennsylvania, where several of his ancestors perished. It contains historic material enough for a volume. To indicate his early passion for amassing reliable data, the same sketch shows that a portion of its facts had been obtained while he was still a boy, from then aged eye witnesses of the affair, nearly fifty years before its story was thus put into permanent shape.

He mastered the Swedish language, after having passed his seventieth year, chiefly that he might write a correct history of the first settlement of Swedes on the Delaware River below Philadelphia. At the age of seventy-two he spent several months in Stockholm, the capital of Sweden, and while there placed himself in communication with every prominent librarian of the country, besides scholars in Denmark, Holland, and Germany. He personally inspected a great mass of documents and ancient volumes. Yet the result of all this is contained in a manuscript of less than thirty large folio pages, literally crowded with invaluable data. This was read before the Historical Society of the State of Delaware in 1874. It has never been put in type, and is almost wholly made up of material which has no existence elsewhere in the English language.

A single instance will serve to show the minuteness and persistence of his investigations. In one of the public libraries of Stockholm Mickley discovered an ancient Dutch manuscript signed by Peter Minuit. No scholar within reach could master its contents. The private secretary of the Ambassador from Holland, who was appealed to, asserted beforehand that he "could read anything that ever was written in Dutch." Yet, after a long inspection, he frankly owned his inability to decipher a single word of it. Mr. Mickley was determined to ascertain the contents. As the document could not be bought at any price, and could not even be removed over night from its place of keeping, he caused photographs to be taken of it. One such copy was sent to a very learned acquaintance in Amsterdam, and another to a noted scholar at Leipzig. In the course of subsequent travels he found accurate translations awaiting him from both sources. The importance of the manuscript in this connection will be the more appreciated when it is remembered that Peter Minuit commanded the first expedition ever sent to the shores of the Delaware River.

Being thus by nature an historian, it is but natural that Mr. Mickley should have left behind him ample materials for telling the story of his own life. From these we learn that the family name was originally Michelet. It dates back to the French Huguenots who, after the revocation of the Edict of Nantes, settled in Zweibrücken, a German province. The first foothold of the family in this country was established in that portion of Pennsylvania which has for more than a century been thickly peopled by that enlightened and art-fostering sect, the Moravians. It was from the Moravian influence that Joseph J. Mickley first experienced a fondness for music and its appropriate artistic surroundings. He was born March 24th, 1799, at South Whitehall, a township then in Lehigh County, but originally comprised in Northampton. At the age of seventeen he went to Philadelphia as apprentice to a pianomaker. At that time the method of building a piano-forte was as different from the advanced art of these days as was the instrument itself. The pianomaker had then to work from the legs upward. His necessary duties demanded knowledge which is now distributed among several entirely distinct sets of artificers. That young Mickley satisfactorily completed his apprenticeship may be inferred from two facts: he started in business for himself in August, 1822, and in October, 1831, the Franklin Institute awarded him a prize for skill in the manufacture of pianos.

From this time on, his business life, though of long duration, was uneventful, and may be summed up in very few words. From his original starting place at No. 67 North Third street, he removed, four years later, to a store on the site now occupied by a portion of the publishing house of J. B. Lippincott Company. Here he remained until 1842, and then established himself in the building mentioned at the beginning of this article, where he continued to live until the final closing up of his business in 1869.

It does not appear that Mr. Mickley was ever actively engaged in the manufacture of piano-fortes. He continued, however, to tune pianos to the end of his life; and it is reported that he could never be induced to alter his terms from the original fee of one dollar, which was customary forty years ago. He also became noted far and wide as a repairer of violins and other stringed instruments. At one time, a violin which had belonged to George Washington, was sent to him for this purpose. Ole Bull, who happened to be in town at the time, hearing of the circumstance, hastened to the shop for the purpose of examining and playing upon the historic instrument. Mickley also became an authority in regard to the value and authenticity of these instruments, although he never indulged in the passion of making collections in this field. His minuteness of observation was frequently manifested. While stopping at Venice in 1870 he notes down in his diary, "A man came to the hotel with some violins for sale. Among them was a Hieronymus Amati. It was a good one, but the head and neck were not genuine." At another time, a violin was sent to his place from a distant locality for repairs. The instrument was preceded by a lengthy letter beseeching his special care for its welfare, and setting forth in extravagant terms its great intrinsic value and its peculiarly interesting "belongings." Anticipating a treasure, Mr. Mickley sent for some violin connoisseurs to enjoy with him a first sight of the precious instrument. On opening the express package a very worthless "fiddle" was revealed. After the laugh had gone round, he said drily, "I think the value of this must be in its 'belongings.'"

In the old house on Market Street, Mr. Mickley was not alone popular among prominent people from afar. He was equally loved by his neighbors on all sides. Many of the more unconventional of these knew him best by the familiar title of "Daddy." To the better educated class of young musicians he was almost as much a father as a friend. Nor were his close friendships confined to the young. Among his most steadfast admirers was an old bachelor German musician by the name of Plich. Herr Plich was a piano teacher, and it was under his tuition that the afterward favorite prima-donna, Caroline Richings made her first public appearance as a pianist in 1847. This old teacher induced Mickley to take him as a boarder, and he lived for a number of years in one of the upper back rooms of No. 927. One night a fire broke out in a building directly contiguous with the rear of the Mickley mansion. There was great consternation, of course, and busy efforts on the owner's part to gather together the manifold contents of his treasure-house. When all had been at length secured in a place of safety, he bethought himself of Herr Plich. Hastening to the upper room, he discovered the old man in a state of semi-insanity, marching up and down the apartment, and carrying in his hands only a valuable viola. So confused was he with fright that main force was required to get him out of the room. After seeing him safely out of the front door, Mickley went back and secured a considerable sum of paper money which had been totally overlooked for the sake of the beloved viola. Plich at his death bequeathed the viola to Mickley, and it was the only instrument which the latter always refused to part with during his lifetime. The entire savings of Plich were also left in trust to Mickley, to be distributed for such charitable objects as he should consider most worthy, and for about twenty-seven years Mr. Mickley carefully administered this trust.

Mr. Mickley's most remarkable success in life was obtained as a numismatist. His habit of collecting coins began almost in childhood. It has been stated that at the age of seventeen he first became interested in coin hunting, owing to his difficulty in finding a copper cent coined in 1799, the year of his birth. Every student of numismatism knows that this piece is exceedingly rare. The one sold in Mr. Mickley's collection after his decease brought no less than forty dollars. The taste thus formed continued a prevailing one for sixty years. It is surprising to find how speedily he became a leading and recognized authority. Although as guileless as a child and the easy victim of numerous thefts throughout his life, he was scarcely ever deceived in the value of a coin, token, or medal. Once, at Stockholm, in 1871, he visited a museum where rare coins were exhibited. "The collection," says his diary, "is very, very rich in Greek and Roman, but particularly in Scandinavian and Anglo-Saxon. There are not many United States coins, but among them I was astonished to find a very fine half-eagle of 1815." The known rarity of this coin thus on exhibition in a far country very naturally attracted the keen eyes of the aged collector.

These researches, continuing year after year, grew to be more and more valuable, until they became widely celebrated. By the time he had reached middle age he was as well known among the guild of antiquarians as a Quaker is known by his costume. Before his death he had been elected a member of all the prominent societies in numismatics, history, and archaeology throughout the world. The last honor of this kind, which reached him in his eightieth year, was a notice of his election to membership in the Société Française de Numismatique et d'Archéologie. His great collections in this department of knowledge were not confined to coins, but extended also to the literature of the subject. This was splendidly illustrated in his famous library, which comprised many works of the utmost value and scarcity,

A taste thus developed in early youth naturally became in the course of years a habit, a sentiment, a leading passion of Mickley's nature. By the year 1867, his coin collection had become the most extensive in the country. By this time also the entertainment of curious visitors absorbed a good share of the collector's daily duties. He was naturally proud of his treasures, and took a great delight in showing them to all who came. Utterly devoid of suspicion, he was a ready victim to designing persons. The following memorandum, which was found among his later papers, will show how he suffered from this source:

"I have become rather indifferent about numismatics, or, at least, about collecting coins. It was a great source of amusement for a period of over fifty years. But having been so unfortunate at different times with my coins, it is, as it were, a warning to desist from collecting any more. In the year 1827, the United States dollars from 1794 to 1803, all good specimens, together with some foreign coins, were stolen. In 1848 about twenty half-dollars were taken. In 1854, after showing my collection to three Southern gentlemen (as they called themselves), I missed three very scarce half-eagles. The great robbery was in 1867. In Jaffa, Palestine, a small lot, worth about one thousand francs, with a collection of Egyptian curiosities, was stolen at the hotel; and, finally, last winter, at Seville, Spain, some old Spanish coins were missing while I was showing them to some persons."

The "great robbery" above alluded to, occurred on the evening of April 13, 1867. It was of such magnitude as to cause a wide sensation at the time, and enlisted the sympathies of his coin hunting brethren the world over. Mr. Mickley's chief precautions, notwithstanding his previous warnings of danger from another source, had been against fire. In a third story room was his cabinet. This had long since been filled, chiefly with an unbroken and historic list of American coins. The additional accumulations of years, nearly all foreign, and many of great rarity, had been stored in an old piano case in his bedroom, where, as he said, in the event of fire they would be close at hand. On the evening in question Mickley was alone in his workshop, engaged in repairing a musical instrument. He had then been living entirely alone for a number of years. A single servant, who provided his meals, had gone home. About nine o'clock the loud barking of his dog in the yard below called him to the window. It was afterward found that a pair of old shoes thrown from an upper room by the burglars had thus called away the attention both of dog and master from what was going on inside. An hour later a caller discovered several pieces of money lying in the hall. An investigation disclosed the startling loss which he had sustained. The entire contents of the piano-box had been carried off. A private desk had also been broken open and despoiled of a few medals, although its chief contents were intact. A gold pencil, the gift of Ole Bull, and other keepsakes, remained undisturbed. But the larger portion of a collection of foreign coins, one of the most complete in the world, and the product of a lifetime's intelligent research, was gone!

It was a heavy calamity, and one from which the old collector never fully recovered. Sir Isaac Newton's historic Fido did not do nearly the amount of irremediable damage when he overturned the lamp upon his master's papers. The actual pecuniary loss, reckoning at cost prices, was in the neighborhood of nineteen thousand dollars. The market value of such a collection was of course vastly greater, and increasing all the time at a good deal faster rate than compound interest. It was somewhat of a coincidence that Mr. Mickley had received and refused what he records as a "tempting offer" for the entire collection only a short time before the robbery.

The ardent passion of a lifetime was now chilled, and his one desire seemed to be to get rid of his remaining coins and of the responsibility which keeping them entailed. Such, however, was the completeness of Mickley's literary methods of condensing, that an entry of three or four lines made in his diary on the night of the robbery is all that he had to write about the appalling loss. A week or two afterward he records in the same volume the disposal of all the remaining coins, with an air of great relief, as he adds, "I do not doubt I should be robbed again if I kept them." A large box full of the most valuable had been taken for safe-keeping, to the Mint just after the robbery; but these were sold with the rest. It is understood that this remnant of the original lot was disposed of for about sixteen thousand dollars, the largest purchaser being Mr. Woodward, of Roxbury, Massachusetts. The dollar of 1804 went to a New York collector for the enormous sum of seven hundred and fifty dollars.

Efforts to restore the lost treasure were not wanting. It might be supposed that the possession of such rare tokens of value would have speedily led to the discovery of their whereabouts. Mr. Mickley himself intimated that he suspected the quarter from which the depredation had come. Yet from that day until the present the secret has been as securely kept as that of the rifling of Lord Byron's letter from a vase at Abbotsford, or of the Duchess of Devonshire's portrait from the London Art Gallery. In fact, the same mild generosity which had always characterized Mr. Mickley still came uppermost in the face of this trying disaster. He frequently sought to overlook the misdoings of petty thieves. A London pickpocket who had successfully practiced upon him Oliver Twist's little game was only prosecuted because his testimony was insisted upon by the authorities. At the foot of the Pyramids he deplored the chastisement inflicted by an Arab sheik upon one of his native servants who had committed a similar depredation. His life-long friend the late William E. Dubois, of the United States Mint, has stated that "eight or nine years after the robbery a few very fine gold pieces of English coinage were offered for sale at the Mint cabinet rooms. I was so well convinced that the labels were in his handwriting that I sent for him to come and see them. He could not deny the likeness, but seemed reluctant to entertain the subject at all."

During these years of study and research, Mr. Mickley must not be thought of as a strict specialist. Side by side with his fascinating collection of coins, there was an ever-growing library, the extent and value of which were never appreciated until his death. This accumulation was in itself an example of his cosmopolitan tastes. It was copious in local history, in biography, in music, in general literature, in costly and well-preserved black-letter editions, in illuminated missals dating back to the thirteenth century, and, above all else, in autographs. Of the latter, space cannot be spared here for anything approaching a full description. As some indication of their value, it may be mentioned that a letter of George Washington (the last he was known to write), dated six days before his death, was bought by George W. Childs, Esq., for one hundred and fifteen dollars. A letter of Abraham Lincoln to General McClellan fetched nearly one hundred dollars. There were also signed autograph letters of all the governors of Pennsylvania, of all the Presidents, and of all the signers of the Declaration of Independence. The latter group is rarely met with complete; and three of the scarcest names alone sold for as much as all the others put together. There were signatures also of about forty generals of the Revolutionary war, of both the British and American armies, and including

Lafayette and Kosciusko. Both Napoleon and Josephine were represented; and the lovers of poetic justice will be glad to know that the latter name brought double that of the great emperor. In autographs of literary and musical celebrities the collection was extraordinarily rich, those of Goethe and Schiller, Beethoven and Mozart, being conspicuous. But the chief rarety was a large album formerly owned by Babet von Ployer. This contained, among other treasures, a manuscript of Haydn, believed to be the only one ever offered for sale in this country. It also contained an India-ink sketch of Mozart, drawn by his wife Constance. At the sale in 1878 this album was knocked down for one hundred and twenty-six dollars, although three hundred dollars had been previously refused for it. The Mozart letter, a particularly interesting specimen, was sold for fifty-two dollars to M. H. Cross, Esq.

Turning from the autographs to the books, we find still greater value and variety. The historical portion, especially where it referred to local subjects, was almost phenomenal. One precious lot comprised a complete set of the first daily newspaper of the United States, beginning with the "Pennsylvania Packet" in 1771, and continuing unbroken, through several changes of title and proprietorship, for one hundred and seven years. An amusing incident is related in connection with Mr. Mickley's purchase of the larger portion of this series, — "Poulson's Advertiser" from 1800 to 1840. When the wagon was driven to his door, loaded with the purchase, the housekeeper exclaimed, "What ever is to be done with all this truck?" Yet this "truck," a mine of wealth to the future historian, was sold after Mickley's death for eight hundred dollars. There were city directories of several editions for ninety-three years. The black-letter list was quite large, and there were more than thirty editions of the Bible, some of great rarity, and nearly all in a fine state of preservation.

From the time of the coin robbery the older acquaintances of Mr. Mickley noticed a decided change in him. On the subject of coins, once so voluble, he grew very reticent. His business, which had for many years appeared rather a pastime than a task to him, grew irksome. After a period of uncertainty, he finally decided to close up his affairs and spend some years in foreign travel. In spite of advanced age, he was both physically and mentally well equipped for such a journey. His health had always been good. His temper seemed never to be ruffled. Of the French and German languages he was a master, and he had some knowledge of the Spanish, Italian, and Swedish. His previous extensive acquaintance with men of many nations and habits was kept fresh in mind by a remarkable memory. With all these advantages, the period of his travels was the most interesting of his life.

Mr. Mickley set sail on the 5th of June, 1869, being at that time a few months past his seventieth year. He remained abroad for three years, visiting every country in Europe, ascending the Nile to the first cataract, passing through the Suez Canal, and across a portion of Asia Minor and Palestine. He made two trips to Northern Sweden to behold the spectacle of the midnight sun. Being a week too late on the first season, he tried it again the following year. Passing through the entire length of the Gulf of Bothnia, and ascending the Tornea River, he entered Lapland, crossing the Arctic circle and penetrating the Arctic zone in a sledge-journey of seventy miles. The indomitable old traveler pushed on until he reached a small lumber-village named Pajala. On the night of June 23, 1871, crossing the river with a small party of Swedes and Finns, he ascended Mount Avasaxa, in Finland. At this altitude, he says, "the sky happened to be clear in the direction of the sun, and he shone in all his glory as the clock struck twelve."

During this prolonged absence he visited almost every considerable town in Germany, Holland, Italy, and England. The instant he arrived at a town, he seemed to know the shortest cut to its museum. If there was an antiquarian in the place, he knew of it beforehand, and hastened either to make or renew an acquaintance. In the larger cities he was surrounded by these people, and he expressed unaffected surprise and pleasure at their attentions. He made visits of inspection to nearly every mint in Europe, having been commissioned by the Philadelphia Mint to make purchases of rare coins for its cabinet. Here the old passion appears to have blazed up again for a little while. It was an entire surprise to his family to discover among his possessions at his death the nucleus of a new collection, which was sold for about two thousand dollars.

Mr. Mickley made at this period some valued acquaintances. Among these was the Italian composer, Mercadante. At the time of Mickley's visit, in April, 1870, the composer, who was also president of the Conservatoire in Naples, had been blind for eight years. "The old gentleman," says Mickley (who, by the way, was only two years his junior), "held out his hand and bade me welcome, I told him it would be a lasting pleasure to have shaken hands with so highly distinguished a man, whose name had long since been favorably known in America. At this his face brightened; he arose from the sofa, shook my hand cordially, wishing me health, happiness, and a safe voyage." Later, at Brussels, he called on M. Fetis, the famous French musical critic and biographer. At that time, in his eighty-eighth year, Fetis was a fugitive from Paris, owing to the troubles of the Franco-Prussian war. Mr. Mickley's picture of the veteran *littérateur* and critic is an engaging one. He says, "Considering his great age, Mr. Fetis is very active. He climbed up the step-ladder to get books and to show me such as he considered the most rare and interesting. He is not only active in body, but he retains all the faculties of his mind. He appears to have a very happy disposition. While I was with him a continual smile was on his face, and it seemed to give him great pleasure to show me his books. He has been engaged in collecting them for over fifty years, and they have cost him a sum equal to three hundred thousand dollars, exclusive of a great many presents. The first book on music was printed in 1480," At Trieste he spent some time with the United States Consul there, Mr. Thayer, of Boston, best known to musical and literary people as the author of an exhaustive Life of Beethoven, which has been under way for nearly thirty years and is not yet finished. Mr. Thayer showed his visitor all the historic data and personal relics which he had collected for the book, of which at that date only one volume had been published. Since then Mercadante and Fetis have been gathered to their fathers. Their genial guest is also gone. The industrious Mr. Thayer lives, with three volumes of the Life completed, and every American, either literary or musical, will wish him well on to the conclusion of his *magnum opus.*

Mr. Mickley's plain personal habits remained almost unchanged by the many unforeseen exigencies of foreign travel. Once, at Rouen, six months after leaving home, he says, "Tasted wine for the first time in Europe, as the water here did not agree with me." A little later, at Munich, he remarks, "Drank beer for the first time." His pockets remained as accessible as heretofore to the nimble fingered gentry. Upon his first visit to Naples, he records very naively, "Three silk handkerchiefs have been stolen from me here, — which is one more than in London." At Jaffa, on his way from Egypt to Palestine, besides the robbery of coins alluded to some time back, he lost a choice autograph manuscript of Mozart which had cost him two hundred and fifty francs at Salzburg. If careless in these particulars, he was very watchful and jealous of opportunities to uphold America's position in the world. He took special pains to inform the mint-masters at various points concerning the superior appliances and machinery of the Philadelphia Mint. On the way back from Lapland, while steaming southward along the upper waters of the Gulf of Bothnia, he writes, under date of July 4, 1871, "This being our national holiday, I put up my flag on the door of my berth, but was obliged to explain the meaning of the holiday to nearly all the passengers." While in England, he met at Manchester a barrister who had formerly been his guest in Philadelphia. This gentleman proposed to introduce him to an American lawyer then practising there. "I asked the name. He said it was Judah P. Benjamin, I declined the invitation."

Wherever Mr. Mickley journeyed, so long as any fresh acquisition of knowledge was to be gained the old traveler appeared insensible to fatigue. When half-way up the Great Pyramid an English group who were in his company stopped and insisted upon going no farther. He resolutely continued, and they, unwilling to see so aged a man out-distance them, followed reluctantly, until all reached the summit and congratulated each other on the famous view. In St. Petersburg, Moscow, and other Russian cities, which he visited in the winter season, he was equally untiring and undaunted. As a specimen of his accuracy of observation, he writes during his first journey in Italy, "I counted forty-six tunnels between Pisa and Bologna." Several severe accidents fell to his lot. In Rome, while exploring a dark arched passage, he fell into "Cicero's Well," receiving severe bruises. In a street in Constantinople, where there are no sidewalks, he was knocked down by a runaway horse and taken up for dead, remaining insensible for several hours. The former of these mishaps occupies three lines in his diary; the latter, twelve lines. On his third visit to Leipzig he was confined in his room for several weeks with an attack of the smallpox. But in regard to none of these accidents, although an aged man, thousands of miles from home, and entirely alone, does he betray any symptoms of apprehension. He merely adds, on the date of his recovery from the attack at Leipzig, "This sickness has detained me much longer than I had expected to stay."

In one of Mickley's trips he made a not unimportant contribution to musical history. Almost every student of instrumental music is acquainted with the name of Jacob Steiner or Stainer, the most successful of violin makers outside of the Cremonese school of workmen. Of Steiner's life but little is known, and no biography of him extant in either French, German, or English contains either the date or place of his death. The account commonly given is that he separated from his wife and died in a convent. Mr. Mickley, with his accustomed perseverance, started out to see if this matter might not be cleared up. At Innspruck he inquired in vain for information. As Fetis and Foster both fixed his birthplace at Absom, a small village some twelve miles from Innspruck, Mickley repaired thither. For some time his errand was fruitless. He stopped in at a little shop where an old woman sold photographs, etc. "I asked her, 'Did you never hear of Jacob Steiner, the violin maker?' She replied, 'There is no Steiner nor violin maker living in this town.' I then said that a celebrated violin maker of that name, of whom I desired some information, had lived there two hundred years before. She replied, quite seriously, 'I am not two hundred years old.'" A few minutes later, in the course of his walk, his eye fell upon an old church, the outer wall of which contained a number of stone tablets with inscriptions. A search of five minutes revealed the desired information. On a plain tablet Steiner's name was found, together with the information, given in very old fashioned German, that he had died there in 1683, "at the rising of the sun."

The closing field of Mr. Mickley's travels covered Southern France and Spain, Lisbon, where he passed the winter of 1871-72, and Madrid. The weather being very severe, he was detained two months at Lisbon, where he engaged a teacher and took daily lessons in Portuguese. He had done the same at Stockholm the previous winter with the Swedish language, which he mastered pretty thoroughly. At Madrid he examined what he emphatically pronounced the finest collection of coins in the world, numbering one hundred and fifty thousand specimens. He adds, "This is the only place in Europe where the subject is properly understood. Alfonzo V., King of Aragon, in the fifteenth century, was the first person known to have collected coins for study or amusement, and Augustin, Archbishop of Tarragona, was the first writer on the subject. The science of numismatics is, therefore, of Spanish origin."

Mr. Mickley left Madrid in March, crossing the Pyrenees and arriving in Paris on the 24th of that month, his seventy-third birthday. He "made the tour of three hundred add sixty-three miles in twelve hours, without being in the least fatigued." After a few weeks passed in Paris and in revisiting friends in England, he sailed for home, arriving in Philadelphia June 5, 1872, exactly three years from the date of his departure.

It was surprising to his friends how little change the lapse of years and the somewhat rugged incidents of travel had made in Mr. Mickley. He quickly settled down, and, as nearly as possible, resumed his old habits. He bought himself a residence, but followed the Paris custom of taking his meals elsewhere. In the house he was entirely alone, even without a servant. After a time he showed some disposition to concede to "luxuries" which he had previously ignored. Carpets he had never used in his life, but he now admitted that they were very pleasant and comfortable, and ordered his house carpeted throughout. The arrangement of his library in the new quarters was a great pleasure, and took some time. Mr. Mickley was in no sense of the word a politician, but he voted pretty regularly. An incident connected with his last visit to the polls was amusing. Having been three years absent, a patriotic Hibernian, who kept the window-book and knew nothing of him, demanded to see his tax receipt. The old gentleman went quietly home and brought back the desired document. He was next asked if he could read and write, which question, however, was not pressed. The last scene in Mr. Mickley's life was as quiet and peaceful as its whole tenor had been. On the afternoon of February 15, 1878, Mr. Carl Plagemann, the well-known musician and friend of many years' standing, called at his house. While he waited, Mr. Mickley wrapped for him some violin strings, the last work of his hands. He requested Mr. Plagemann to go with him that evening to visit another old friend, — Oliver Hopkinson, Esq., at whose house there were to be some quartettes. "I have a letter," he said, "from the Russian Ambassador, a part of which I am unable to translate. A Russian lady is to play the piano there this evening, and I shall ask her to help me out." Mr. Plagemann could not go, and, as so often before, Mr. Mickley started out alone. Just before reaching the house of Mr. Hopkinson he was taken suddenly ill, and, chancing to be close by the residence of his physician. Dr. Meigs, he stopped there and rang the bell. As the door opened, he said in husky tones, "I am suffocating." He walked in and ascended the stairs without assistance. Then he said, "Take me to a window." As this was being done, he fell back insensible into the arms of the attendants, and, a few minutes later, breathed his last.

Thus, on the very western edge of fourscore years, ended this long and industrious, this peaceful and beautiful life. In our land of busy and constant action there have been few like it — surely none happier. Serene at the close as it was placid in its course, its lot had been cast ever between quiet shores, which it enriched on either hand with its accumulated gifts of knowledge and taste. And at the close of it all there could be no happier eulogy than the one modestly yet comprehensively delivered by his old and congenial friend William E. Dubois, himself since summoned to take the same mysterious journey. "In fine," says he, "Mr. Mickley seemed superior to any meanness; free from vulgar passions and habits, from pride and vanity, from evil speaking and harsh judging. He was eminently sincere, affable, kind, and gentle; in the best sense of the word he was a gentleman."

Obituaries

OF A FEW OF THE MEMBERS OF THE MICKLEY FAMILY OF WHOM A RECORD HAS BEEN COMPILED

These obituaries, which are mainly newspaper sketches, were in the possession of the compiler, and it was thought that they might prove of interest to the family.

JACOB MICKLEY, 38.

DEATH OF JACOB MICKLEY, THE LAST SURVIVOR IN LEHIGH COUNTY, OF THE WAR OF 1812

Jacob Mickley, commonly regarded as the oldest male resident of Lehigh county, died on Saturday afternoon at two o'clock at his home at Mickley's, aged ninety-four years, two months, and six days. He had been in rather feeble health for several years, but it was not until a short time ago that he began to fail at a rate that led his children and friends to feel that the end was near. There was no organic disease — simply the wearing out incident to extreme old age. March 27th last, at the celebration of his ninety-fourth anniversary, he was bright, cheerful, and reminiscent, surrounded by children, grandchildren, great-grandchildren, and friends, to whom he related interesting events of the long ago. All his faculties were well preserved until the end.

The Late Jacob Mickley, of Mickleys, Pa.

John Jacob Mickley, the great-grandfather of Jacob Mickley, was a native of Alsace, and, with a company of Huguenots, emigrated to America to escape religious persecution. He had four sons — John

Jacob, John Martin, John Peter and Henry. The first named, the grandfather of the subject of this sketch, was born in what is now Lehigh county, and married Miss Susan Miller. Their eldest son, Jacob, married Miss Eva Catharine Schreiber. Their children were Jacob, Joseph J., Polly (Mrs. Daniel Moyer), Sarah (Mrs. John Schwartz) and Anna (Mrs. Andrew Sheldon). The father, who was a volunteer during the famous whiskey insurrection in Pennsylvania, spent his life in farming occupations in Whitehall township, and died at the home of his son, Jacob, in 1857, in the ninety-first year of his age.

Jacob Mickley, the subject of this biography, was born on March 27th, 1794, on the homestead farm, and devoted his whole life to the pursuits of agriculture. The educational advantages in those days were limited, and after the meagre opportunities of the home school had been taken advantage of, he attended for a brief period a school in Warren county, New Jersey. At the early age of twelve he became familiar with all manner of farm work, which in those days was far more laborious than in these days of agricultural labor-saving machinery. When war was declared between Great Britain and America in 1812, his youthful patriotism was stirred and he enlisted, and with his Lehigh county colleagues did duty at Marcus Hook and other historical places. He was the last survivor in Lehigh county of the war of 1812. His memory of the stirring events of those days was clear and he loved to dwell on the scenes and incidents of that struggle. In 1826 he purchased the homestead farm, which he continued to cultivate until 185 1, when he built the residence in which he died. Mr. Mickley was married in 1817 to Miss Anna Kern, daughter of Nicholas Kern, of Whitehall. She died in April, 1880. Their surviving children are Mary (Mrs. Valentine W. Weaver, of Macungie); Rebecca (Mrs. Samuel Thomas, of Catasauqua); Eliza (Mrs. Rev. David Kuntz, of Nazareth); Jane (Mrs. Enoch Phillips, of Virginia); Edwin Mickley, of Hokendauqua; William Mickley, of Alburtis, and Catharine Mickley, who resided with her father. The deceased children are Ephraim, James, Lovinia and Francisca. His only surviving sister is Mrs. Sheldon.

Mr. Mickley was an old line Whig in politics and when the Republican party was organized became at once an enthusiastic and devoted adherent. He was largely instrumental in the erection of what is known as "Mickley's Church." Of a kind and helpful disposition, he was ever ready to contribute to religious and charitable objects. He was of a cheerful nature and loved to be surrounded by his family and friends. He was an interesting link connecting the present with the past and his unclouded memory of events of the long ago made him a most companionable man. He voted at every Presidential election since 1S16. The funeral will take place on Thursday afternoon at two o'clock from his late residence. Services and interment at Mickley's Church.

ANNA KERN-MICKLEY, 38.

On Wednesday last the remains of Anna, the wife of Mr. Jacob Mickley, residing at Mickley's, in Whitehall, were consigned to their last resting place in the quiet church yard near the family residence, in the presence of a very large concourse of mourning relatives and sorrowing friends. It was one of the largest funerals ever held in the township. Seldom has grief been so generally sincerely expressed as marked this funeral occasion, and the manifestations of sorrow given out must have been to the bereaved a source of some consolation. The death of Mrs. Mickley occurred on the 27th ultimo, after a lingering illness under the infirmities of her years — she having attained the age of eighty-three years, nine months and eight days. She was the mother of eleven children, nine of whom survive, among them Messrs. Ephraim Mickley, of this city, and James W., and Edwin Mickley, of Hokendauqua. Deceased was a sincere and devout Christian, a kind and obliging neighbor and friend, a fond and devoted wife and mother. What higher eulogy than this; what more could be said. She has gone to her reward, and left behind a bright and shining example. Her departure carries profound regret and sorrow to a very large circle of acquaintances. All who knew her were her friends, both young and old having been attached to her by her cheerful disposition and unvarying kindness. She was a consistent member of the Reformed church, and her Christian character was always manifested in her daily life. She was especially noted for her goodness of heart, gentleness of spirit, and her generous treatment of the unfortunate poor. A good woman, and a Christian in every sense of the word, her life is an example for all to follow. The bereaved aged husband and children have our earnest sympathies along with those of the community. At the funeral Revs. W. R. Hofford, J. D. Schindel and J. A. Little pronounced -appropriate discourses.

SUSAN MICKLEY-BIERY, 22.

Susan, wife of the late Frederick Biery, another of a past generation, has gone from us to her eternal home. She was the mother of the late Peter Biery. She died at the home of her granddaughter, Mrs. Eliza Lightcap, cor. Ninth and Walnut streets. She was the daughter of John Martin Mickley, and was born in Whitehall Township in 1773. Allentown was then a village, having been laid out in 1762.

Mrs. Biery had nine children, one hundred grandchildren, and eighty-eight great-grandchildren, and fourteen great-great-grandchildren. She was blind for some years before her death.

ANNA MICKLEY-SHELDON, 40.

WIFE OF THE LATE ANDREW SHELDON

Mrs. Anna Sheldon, of Mickleys, died on Wednesday of last week, aged ninety-three years, six months, and nineteen days; her death resulted from La Grippe and the infirmities of age. Deceased was the widow of Andrew Sheldon and was a member or a family noted for its longevity. Her brother,

Jacob Mickley, died a few years ago at the age of ninety-four years. Her father was ninety-two when he died, and her mother lived to the age of eighty-eight.

Mrs. Sheldon was twice married; her first husband was John Youndt; and of their four children the only survivor is Mrs. Sarah Rau, of Bethlehem, Pa. By her second husband she had four children, all of whom are living, namely, Lewis Sheldon, of Allentown; John M. Sheldon, of Philadelphia; Edmund M. Sheldon, of Hughesville, Pa. Her descendants numbered eight children, seventeen grandchildren, fifteen great-grandchildren and three great-great-grandchildren. She lived to see five generations in her home.

PETER MICKLEY, 42.

Peter Mickley, a resident of North Whitehall Township, died yesterday, February 20th, 1877, in the eightieth year of his age. He was one of the most widely known citizens of Lehigh county, and was greatly esteemed as an honorable and useful man. He leaves a widow and three sons and one daughter. Abraham, Frank, Alfred, and Mrs. Francis Levan, of Coplay.

MARY MICKLEY-SNYDER, 48.

ALMOST A CENTURY.

Mary M. Snyder, relict of the late Daniel Snyder, Sr., died on Monday at two o'clock in the afternoon. She was seized with an attack of illness on Tuesday of last week, which the attending physician, Dr. Harter, pronounced lesion of the brain. This resulted in paralysis of the right side on Monday morning, and she gradually sank until the final change, which came painlessly and peacefully. The funeral took place on Thursday afternoon at three o'clock.

Mrs. Snyder was the oldest old-time resident of Bloomsburg. She was born in Allentown, Pa., April 2, 1792, making her age ninety-seven years, three days. She was the daughter of Peter Mickley and Sarah Biery Mickley. Peter Mickley was a grandson of John Jacob Mickley, or Michelet, who came from Rotterdam, Holland, in the ship "Hope," of London, arriving in Philadelphia, August 28, 1733.

Mary Mickley married Daniel Snyder in 1809, and in 1810 he came to Columbia county and bought twenty-six acres of land, now mostly in the built up portion of Bloomsburg, paying for the same £550. His intention was to erect a tannery, and he selected a site for it at what is now the corner of Main street and the Lightstreet road, on account of the run that would supply the tannery with water, but he was greatly discouraged on being told that this stream would sometimes run dry, and he for a while contemplated giving up his claim. They were living at Easton at that time, 1810, and Mr. Snyder becoming convinced that the supply of water was unfailing, employed Squire Hutchison to haul him, with his family and goods to Bloomsburg. They settled in a little log cabin which stood where he afterwards erected the capacious brick mansion still occupied by the family, on the corner of Main and East streets. Mr. Snyder met with some business discouragements, but his pluck and energy carried him through, and in ten years he was able to build a two-story brick house, which afterwards was converted into a hotel, and was known as the "Forks Hotel."

It stood at the foot of what is now Normal Hill, and was then at the head of Main street. It was erected about 1825, and was removed in 1875, after the building of the Institution and the opening up of Main street to the school. He prospered in business, became the owner of a large tannery, valuable town property, and five or six farms. He represented this county in the legislature from 1840 to 1844.

Mr. and Mrs. Snyder were the parents of ten children, as follows: William, Sarah A., who married Dr. William Petriken; Melvina, who married Elisha Barton; Polly, Daniel, Matilda, who married Rev. Henry Funk; Mary C, who married Dr. F. C. Harrison; Martha Alice, who married Dr. T. C. Harter; and Clinton B. Snyder. Of these, only Mrs. Petriken, Mrs. Barton, Daniel Snyder, and Mrs. Harter survive.

There are living seven grandchildren, who are the following: N. U. Funk, Esq., Mrs. Gen. W. H. Ent, Mrs. F. P. Billmeyer, Mrs. Alice John, Mrs. Dr. Lazarus, Clinton C. Snyder and Mrs. W. B. Milnes. Mrs. C. W. Neal, deceased, was a granddaughter of Mrs. Snyder. There are living sixteen great-grandchildren.

Mrs. Snyder was a woman of equable temperament, always cheerful and pleasant, a devoted Christian woman, being for many years a member of the Reformed Church. For nearly eighty years she lived in Bloomsburg, and saw the place gradually develop from a mere country hamlet to its present proportions. There are but few who have lived so long, or whose birth occurred in the eighteenth century, and soon they must pass away and the earth shall know them no more. Mrs. Snyder possessed all her faculties in a remarkable degree, her only apparent weakness being loss of memory. It was a pleasure to talk with her, and listen to the reminiscences of the early days which she was wont to tell. She has gone to her reward, and she leaves the memories of a long and useful life.

EDWARD B. MICKLEY, 61.

The genial presence of our citizen, Mr. Edward B. Mickley, will be sadly missed. For half a century he was a resident of Waterloo. During these years he made many friends who admired his happy disposition, and enjoyed the cordial greeting that he always had for them.

Edward Mickley came to Seneca county when a young man, from North Whitehall, Lehigh county, Pennsylvania, and settled in Fayette. At one time he was supervisor of that town and held several official positions of public trust, discharging the duties faithfully and honorably. For several years he was a grain shipper to Albany and New York, and employed a number of canal boats. Successful in business, he accumulated a fortune, but reverses came which he stood manfully, retaining the confidence and respect of all. Later in life he engaged in the dry goods business and his services were eagerly sought by the merchants in Waterloo. In 1838 he was a member of the firm of Mickley & Kohler, dry goods merchants in South Waterloo. He was afterwards associated with Mr. Seigfried in the flouring business, and subsequently with the late General Markel, in the brick mills in South Waterloo. Deceased was seventy-six years of age. He had a high sense of honor, and was particularly courteous and polite, with a smile and a kind word for all. He was an affectionate parent and loved his family, and enjoyed the respect of his fellow citizens, and lived a life of happy content. He leaves a family of nine children; six sons and three daughters, all to womanhood and manhood grown. They mourn the loss with heartfelt sorrow, and have the sympathy of many in their affliction. Mr. Mickley was stricken with paralysis, Thursday, February 5th, and lingered along until Wednesday of last week, February 11th, when he passed away. His funeral was held Saturday afternoon, at his late residence on Elizabeth street.

PETER MICKLEY, 83.

Peter Mickley, one of the oldest and most respected citizens of the county, died in Cashtown, on Tuesday, April 25th, 1893, aged ninety-five years, eleven months, and fifteen days. Mr. Mickley was born on the 11th day of May, 1797, at the old Mickley home on the banks of Little Marsh creek in Franklin township, this county. He always lived in his native township and was a leading citizen, whose opinions and views had the force of a strong individuality and were regarded by his neighbors as sound and conservative.

This family has been a long lived one; his brothers, Abram and Henry, having only preceded him by a few years, also at a ripe old age. Daniel Mickley, the father of Colonel D. W. Mickley, is the only surviving member of this once large family, who is now almost ninety-eight years old and much enfeebled by his extreme age.

REBECCA MICKLEY-THOMAS, 125.

Rebecca, the beloved wife of Mr. Samuel Thomas, died at their temporary home, at six o'clock, on Sunday morning last. For months she had been in ill-health, but on Sunday, 8th inst., her illness assumed a most serious form, and throughout the week the gravest apprehensions were entertained. Dr. M. E. Hornbeck, her attending physician, called to his aid Drs. E. G. Martin and W. L. Estes, of St. Luke's Hospital, and Dr. J. C. Guernsey, her son-in-law, of Philadelphia, were present on several occasions, but all that medical science and loving attendance could do was of no avail. On Sunday her case became hopeless. The invalid was not sufficiently strong to rally from the disease, and lingered, surrounded by loving relatives and friends, until six o'clock A. M., when frail humanity gave up the cares of this world and her spirit took its flight to realms above, mourned by a wide circle of relatives and friends. Her husband, son and daughter were with her in her last hours.

Deceased was a life-long resident of this vicinity; born at Mickleys; her father was the late venerable Jacob Mickley, and was married to Samuel Thomas in March, 1848; one brother, Mr. Edwin Mickley, of Mickleys; four sisters, Mrs. Rev. D. A. Kuntz, of Nazareth; Mrs. Enoch Philips, of Pulaski City, Va.; Mrs. Valentine W. Weaver, of Macungie, and Miss Kate Mickley, of Allentown, survive her. Descending from a celebrated family and by marriage connecting herself with the eldest son of the renowned David Thomas, she has always deservedly held a prominent position in our valley.

She was always an earnest and devoted member of the Presbyterian Church; her husband was the first elder in the Presbyterian Church at Hokendauqua; and she freely gave her time and means to the advancement of that denomination. She was a woman of culture and refinement, being deeply devoted to her family and home. Loved by all her neighbors, her loss will be sadly felt. She was greatly interested in the rebuilding and improvement of their home, Second and Pine streets, in the midst of which alterations, the husband was called to part with his helpmeet in the designs. The funeral took place on Thursday afternoon, short services were held at the house, and the remains conveyed to the First Presbyterian Church, Catasauqua, by the following pall-bearers: Messrs. James Thomas, Charles Corwin, Morgan Emanuel, Daniel Davis, Daniel Milson and James Nevins, life-long friends of the deceased. The church was crowded with friends from all the towns along the valley and distant points. The cortége entered while Professor Prescott, who presided at the organ, rendered Chopin's dirge. The Thomas Quartette, of Hokendauqua, most beautifully rendered the vocal selections. The services throughout were very solemn and impressive. The pastors who took part in the services were Rev. David Harbison, Rev. Dr. Cattell, Rev. Dr. Earle and Rev. Dr. James A. Little. An opportunity was then afforded the large assembly to take a farewell look at the features of one who had long held an affectionate place in the hearts of many of our people. Interment was privately made in the family vault in Fairview Cemetery. Short and impressive services were held at the burial place.

EPHRAIM MICKLEY, 126.

This well-known citizen died on Sunday noon, October 9, 1887, at the residence of Mr. Newhard, at Laury's. He retired Saturday night in his usual health, and when on Sunday morning he did not respond to the call for breakfast, a member of the family rapped at his bedroom door, he was heard to breathe heavily, the door was broken in, medical aid was summoned, but he could not be restored to consciousness and at noon breathed his last. Ephraim Mickley was the eldest son of the venerable Jacob Mickley, who was ninety-three years old last March. The deceased for a number of years owned the Mickley homestead farm, now owned by V. W. Weaver, of Macungie. Pa. After his retirement from the farm, he was in the foundry business in Fogelsville, afterward engaged in the coal and grain business in Allentown. He retired about eighteen years ago and was not engaged in any pursuit. His wife, Elizabeth, *née* Deshler, died in 1872. Mr. Mickley was an earnest uncompromising Republican. The funeral will take place to-morrow afternoon from the residence of his aged father at Mickleys. Services and interment at the Mickley's church.

ELIZABETH A. DESHLER-MICKLEY, 126.

Elizabeth A., wife of Ephraim Mickley, residing on Gordon street near Sixth, died on Sunday evening last, after only a few days illness. Her demise casts a gloom over a large circle of friends and relatives. Verily, "In the midst of life we are in death."

She had but last spring removed with her husband to this city, to await the completion of a new home on North Sixth street, which she had especially arranged for convenience and comfort. But alas, she was summoned before it was ready for occupancy. She first complained of illness on Wednesday, but was not thought seriously ill until Friday. Her ailment was spotted fever. She was the daughter of our long deceased townsman, James Deshler, of Whitehall, and a sister of Jacob, D. J., Frank, and Peter Deshler.

She was a woman whose home and its duties were dear to her heart, of gentle and unaffected manners, amicable disposition, and was held in high esteem by her numerous friends and acquaintances. In her death, her husband has lost a dutiful and loving companion. The community sympathizes with him in his great bereavement. Interment will be made in the Deshler family plot at Egypt, Pa.

JAMES W. MICKLEY, 127.

Lehigh County lost a good citizen and the Republican party an active and influential member this morning (October 16th, 1880), in the death of James W. Mickley, of Hokendauqua, at the age of fifty-three. Mr. Mickley had for years been a great sufferer from asthma, but it was only about four weeks ago that he was confined to bed. His condition the past week left little hope of his recovery. He died this morning at four o'clock, surrounded by his family and a number of friends. His wife and three children survive him. Mr. Mickley for many years was superintendent of the ore beds of the Thomas Iron Company, in which position he rendered the fullest satisfaction to his employers. In 1856 he was Clerk of the Court of Quarter Sessions, and for a time afterward was Teller in the Catasauqua National Bank. In politics he was an ardent Republican, working for and contributing freely towards the success of the party. He served as delegate to State Conventions and a few years ago presided over the Republican County Convention. He was widely known throughout the eastern portion of the State and enjoyed great popularity, and his friends in this city are grieved to learn of his death. The funeral will take place on Tuesday afternoon from his residence at Hokendauqua.

WILLIAM J. MICKLEY, 131.

In Philadelphia, May 16th, 1891, from the effects of the grippe in his fifty-fourth year. He was a prominent citizen of Alburtis, Pa.; an elder in the Presbyterian church. He was the son of the late Jacob and Anna Kern-Mickley, of Mickleys, Pa. He was married to Lucy Keck. One daughter, Stella, a brother, Edwin, and sisters, Mrs. V. W. Weaver, Mrs. Samuel Thomas, Mrs. Enoch Philips, Mrs. David Kuntz and Miss Kate Mickley, survive him. Interment will be privately made at the family burying ground at Mickleys, Pa., May 20th, 1891.

JOSEPHINE C. MICKLEY-JOHNSON, 136.

Josephine C. Mickley, wife of John J. Johnson, died at her home at West Philadelphia, after a short illness. She was the daughter of the late Joseph J., and Cordelia Hopfeldt-Mickley, aged fifty-seven years and eleven months. Deceased was born in Philadelphia, was a noble and beautiful character. Her husband alone is left to mourn her loss. Although her many relatives and friends will feel her loss and mourn for her.

JOHN JACOB MICKLEY, 138.

THE OLD PIONEER SUDDENLY STRICKEN YESTERDAY WITH APOPLEXY

John J. Mickley, an old resident of this city, Visalia, was suddenly stricken with apoplexy yesterday afternoon (December 6th, 1892), about 2.30 o'clock, and after a few minutes struggling finally died. Mr. Mickley has not been well since last Thursday, and has not been in his jewelry shop for several days. He slept all of yesterday morning, getting up about one o'clock. While lying on a lounge in his dining-room he was attacked by the dread malady. Mrs. Mickley sent for Dr. Hall, who arrived quickly, but the unfortunate man was beyond all human aid. He died in a few minutes after the attack.

Mr. Mickley was the son of the late Joseph J. and Diana Blumer-Mickley, and was a native of Philadelphia, Pa. He was born November 23d, 1836, and at his death was fifty-six years old. He came to this county about 1858, after which he moved to Mariposa County, where he remained for several years, finally moving to this city. He has been a resident of Visalia for the past thirty years, and has been engaged in the jewelry business during all that time. The deceased was a singularly quiet man, but had made a host of friends since his residence here, and the news of his death will cause regret wherever he was known. He was a good citizen and a man of sterling character. He married eleven years ago. His death occurring on his eleventh marriage anniversary; his wife was Emma L. Luther. He left no children. The funeral services will take place Friday morning under the auspices of the Visalia Lodge. He was one of the pioneer members of the fire department, but has been on the exempt list for a number of years.

CHARLES MICKLEY, 149.

Captain Charles Mickley was born in Whitehall Township, near Mickleys, January 27th, 1823. He began his business career as clerk for the Trexlers of Long-swamp. Later as Superintendent of the "Paradise furnace," Huntington, Pa., and later Superintendent of the "Rough and Ready" furnace.

During the year 1857 he came to Allentown and was in the milling business until the outbreak of the Civil war. He was Captain of Company G, Forty-seventh Regiment, Pennsylvania Volunteers, and was killed in the battle of Pocotaligo, South Carolina, October 22, 1862. Mr. Wolf, the sutler of the regiment, contrived to send his body with his personal effects through the Southern lines to New York, and had it sent to his family, to whom he telegraphed the news. Charles Mickley was married to Eliza Heinbach, who with five sons and one daughter survive him.

MATHIAS MICKLEY, 155.

The death of Mathias Mickley, which occurred on Saturday morning, although sudden was not unexpected. For several months he had been confined to his room by a complication of kidney and dropsical diseases which almost from the first threatened to be serious. During his sickness he was cheerful and hopeful, although realizing that the end might not be far off. He failed rapidly during Friday night, and in the early morning of Saturday suddenly throwing his hands above his head, breathed his last.

The funeral took place Monday at two o'clock from the court room adjoining the rooms occupied by the family of the deceased. The ceremonies were in charge of the Ancient Order of United Workmen, of which the late Sheriff had been a member, the lodge attending in a body, with a large representation of the Sauk Rapids lodge, and also the J. M. McKelvy Post, G. A. R. The county officers attended in a body, and the local bar was largely represented. The services were conducted by the Rev. E. V. Campbell, pastor of the Presbyterian church — the singing being by a male quartette, Messrs. Smith, Waller, Mills and Hargrave — after which the remains were taken to the Masonic burial grounds, the procession being a large one. The pall bearers were: P. R. Griebler and B. Rensken, St. Cloud Lodge, A. O. U. W.; J. L. Kniskern and Jos. Hoffman, Sauk Rapids Lodge A. O. U. W.; M. C. Moran and J. L. Uptagrove, G. A. R.

Sheriff Mickley was one of the most popular men both personally and politically in Stearns county. His big body contained a big heart, and he numbered his friends by the score in every town and precinct. He leaves a wife and five children, four boys and one girl, the eldest a boy of eleven years and the youngest an infant. The following sketch of his life, the data for which was furnished by himself, is republished from The Journal-Press of January 6, 1887, where it first appeared:

"Mathias Mickley is a Pennsylvanian, and was born in Lehigh county in November, 1833. His father was in the iron ore and furnace business, and after the usual siege at the village school he sent his son to the college at Easton. Young Mat., however, did not take kindly to quiet student life, he wanted something more stirring, and in 1853 he came west, to St. Paul. He worked his own way, taking care of himself, and later he took a trip through the Indian country, being curious to see the aborigines in their own houses. In 1856 he came to St. Cloud and took charge of Col. Lowry's lumber yard for a year, and for the following two years ran it on his own account. In the fall of 1856 he was appointed Deputy Sheriff and was Sheriff when, at the Indian outbreak, he joined the Minnesota Mounted Rangers and went west with Gen. Sibley's expedition. Returning from that trip with a whole skin and his scalp in the place where the scalp ought to be, he enlisted in the Minnesota First and got South in time to see a good deal of stiff fighting and served until the close of the war, when he returned home and was again made Deputy Sheriff, and at the next election was made Sheriff, which office he has retained since with the exception of two years, when he retired to private life and another term as Deputy. In all he has been Sheriff and Deputy about twenty-five years. In August, 1873, he married Miss Augusta Dorr, and they have several children. Sheriff Mickley is a great favorite in Stearns county, and there are a good many voters of both parties whose support he can always count on against any competitor."

COMPILER'S NOTICE

I hope the record will be kept by the members of the family.

It may have been noticed that the date of birth has been omitted in the Fifth and Sixth Generations; it was impossible to get the dates of the last generation, because they are living. It is only the dead whose dates are recorded in the Fifth and Sixth Generations, which idea I hope will be faithfully carried out, and in this way we will have a full record. The space has been left for the insertion of dates. I know this is not the getter al rule for genealogies, but I have tried to make the record in every way acceptable to all the members of the Mickley family. It is hoped that as many as possible will be present at the reunion of the family upon the anniversary of our ancestor's arrival in America, August 27th, 1733, which we hope to celebrate at Mickleys, August 27th, 1894.

Historical Memorabilia

THE LIBERTY BELL EPISODE

The Liberty Bell of Philadelphia, famous as having proclaimed the adoption of the Declaration of Independence on July 4th, 1776, has made two remarkable journeys which are in striking contrast — before the triumphal one to Chicago which has just occurred. The latter one of the two referred to was in January, 1885, to the World's Fair in New Orleans which is oftener recalled as the great Cotton Exposition. On that journey as on the one of the present year, 1893, it was honored in every possible way until its return to Philadelphia in June of the same year.

Its first journey, made in September, 1777, one hundred and eight years earlier, was of a different character. And but few persons were entrusted with the important secret of its removal from the State House or of its destination.

A panel of a large stained glass window adorning the façade of Zion's Reformed Church of Allentown, Pennsylvania, has a representation of the old bell with the following inscription: "In commemoration of the safekeeping of the Liberty Bell in Zion's Reformed Church, A. D., 1777."

It will be remembered that when the British troops invaded Philadelphia the bell was secretly removed for safe-keeping, and that it was loaded on a wagon and carried off, ostensibly with the baggage train of the Continental Army. The impression was given that its sacred and patriotic tongue had forever been drowned in the Delaware river. Some historians say it was taken to Lancaster, Pennsylvania, where Congress repaired in 1777, the same month removing to York, Pennsylvania, where it remained in session until June 27, 1778.

The fact was that in September, 1777, by order of the Executive Council, the State House bell, the bells of Christ Church and St. Peter's Church, eleven bells, were removed to Allentown by way of Bethlehem. This action was taken, it is said, because it was recognized as one of the rights of the captors of a town to seize upon the church bells as spoils of war and transmute them into cannon. After the evacuation of Philadelphia by the British, the bells were brought back and put in their respective places, in the latter part of the year 1778.

The diary of the Moravian Church of Bethlehem, kept by the presiding Bishop, has the following entry under date of September 23, 1777: "The bells from Philadelphia brought in wagons. The wagon with the State House Bell broke down here, so it had to be unloaded; the other bells went on." They were all taken to Allentown and the State House bell and the chimes of Christ Church were buried beneath the floor of Zion's Reformed Church. The Church was built in 1762, of logs, rebuilt of stone in 1770, and again rebuilt later. The Rev. Abraham Blummer was pastor of the Church at the time the bells arrived and assisted in the work of concealing them. His son Henry was married to Sarah, a daughter of John Jacob Mickley, (my great-great-grandfather), who had charge of the bells from Philadelphia to Allentown. He brought them on his wagon, drawn by his own horses. His son, John Jacob, (my great-grandfather), then a boy of eleven years, rode on the wagon which carried the State House bell, and was occasionally allowed to drive. The description, as he gave it, of his first visit and ride to and from Philadelphia, as told to his grandchildren (of whom my father is one), would be an interesting story.

The bells were taken from Philadelphia during the night and had the appearance of farmers' wagons, loaded with manure, the strategy used to conceal them and to insure their safety. The breaking down of the wagon at Bethlehem was a most aggravating delay just six miles from home and four miles from the place where the bells were to be concealed.

John Jacob Mickley, who had charge of the bell, was the son of John Jacques Michelet, a Huguenot refugee of the Michelet family, of Metz, Lorraine, France. The family fled to Deux Ponts, then a German Province, whence the son left for Rotterdam and came to America on the ship Hope, to Philadelphia. On this ship his name was registered Johan Jacob Mueckli. Arriving in Philadelphia he took the oath of allegiance, August 27, 1733, and settled in White Hall, Lehigh County, Pennsylvania, where many of his descendants reside. The name has undergone many changes. In various deeds and other documents in my possession the name is written Michelet, Miquelet, Mueckli, Michley, and finally fell into the present form of Mickley, used during the past four generations. Jean Jacques had three sons, the eldest, John Jacob, who with his large means aided in every way he could the cause of the Continental Army. He gave his teams for its use and his personal assistance in secreting the bells of Philadelphia. John Martin, his brother, was a soldier in the Revolutionary War and was in the battle of Germantown. John Peter, the third brother, served in the capacity of fifer, was in the battle of Germantown and served during the entire Revolutionary war. — *Written for the "American Monthly Magazine" by Minnie F. Mickley.*

Note — Frederick Leiser's wagon was used to convey the State House Bell from Bethlehem to Allentown; when the breakdown occurred his wagon was pressed into service, but whether he accompanied the bell or not, I do not know. His great-grandson furnished me with this interesting item.

II - Extracts From Pennsylvania Archives

The following names of members of the Mickley Family and those whose wives or daughters were Mickleys, are found in the Pennsylvania Archives, Vol. XI-XIV, Second Series. Many of the names of those who fought in the

Revolution from Whitehall Township and Northampton County are not given — none but the officers of the Whitehall Company are given.

Jacob Mickley or John Jacob Mickley, 1. — Jacob Mickley's name appears in Vols. X and XIV of the Pennsylvania Archives. Vol. X, page 765, in the roll of Captain Benjamin Weiser's Company. Commanded by Colonel Nicholas Houseaker, Esq., in the service in the United Colonies. In barracks, Philadelphia, October 3d, 1776. Jacob Mickley, September 1st, 1776. In Vol. XIV, Pennsylvania Archives, page 630: "At a meeting of the General Committee of this County, held at Easton, the 11th of November, A. D., 1776, the following returns were delivered for new members: "The new members for Whitehall were Peter Kohler and Jacob Mickley."

In Vol. XIV, page 596, in a drafted Company, 1781. List of members of Upper Milford township, Northampton County Militia, for the Eighth Class of Colonel Balliet's Battalion (being the First Battalion), 22nd of July, 1781. From Captain Zerfass' (First) Company. Out of the eight Companies, twenty-nine had substitutes, three moved away, three marched in other Companies and twenty-one marched with one of the eight Companies. Jacob Mickley's substitute was Ulrich Arner.

During the summer of 1777, Jacob Mickley gave the use of his horses and wagons, in Conrad Kreider's Wagon Brigade.

Vol. XIV, page 565. — In the Whitehall Company, the Captain was Peter Burkhalter, May 22d, 1775. Total rank and file, 100 men. Peter Burkhalter was the brother of Elizabeth Barbara Burkhalter-Mickley, wife of John Jacob Mickley, who settled in Northampton County in 1733. If the muster roll of this Company could be found, most of the names of those on the assessment roll of Whitehall Township of 1781 could be found in that Company.

Captain Nicholas Kern's Company, July 9th, 1776, composed part of the flying camp of ten thousand men, commanded by Colonel Hart. In 1784, Colonel Nicholas Kern commanded an expedition to Wyoming, Pennsylvania, from Northampton County. Anna Kern-Mickley, wife of Jacob Mickley, 38, was the daughter of Nicholas Kern, of Northampton County, now Lehigh County. Vol. XIV, page 601.

Jacob Schrieber, September 22, 1781, a private in Captain Adam Serfoo's Company, consisting of the First Class of Northampton County Militia, now in the service of the United States, commanded by Col. Christian Shaus. Jacob Schrieber was the father of Eva Catherine Schrieber-Mickley, 8. Vol. XIV.

In the Muster Roll of the Sixth Class of the First Battalion of Northampton County Militia, under command of Lieutenant-Colonel Henry Geiger, November 15th, 1781, is found the name of John Balliet, November 15th, 1781 (Clerk). John Balliet was the husband of Catherine Mickley-Balliet, 16. Vol. XIV, page 598.

In the Committee of Observation, chosen December 21st, 1774, appears David Deshler's name, also Nicholas Kern and Abraham Miller. Vol. XIV, page 563.

At a meeting of the General Committee of the County of Northampton, held at Easton, the 30th of May, A. D., 1776, there were present the following members, being newly elected — For Salisbury, David Deshler and John Gerhart; for Macongie, John Wetzel, George Brenning and John Fogle (Fogel). David Deshler was the father of Elizabeth Deshler-Mickley, who was the wife of Christian Mickley, 9.

Abraham Miller was the father of Susanne MillerMickley, wife of John Jacob Mickley, 1.

John Fogel was the great-grandfather of Matilda Fogel, wife of Edwin Mickley, 128.

It is to be hoped that the muster roll of the Whitehall Company of the Revolution can yet be found and placed in the hands of William H. Egle, M. D., of Harrisburg, for the next volume of Pennsylvania Archives.

Indexes

Index First

The following index contains the names of ail the Mickleys in the preceding catalogue, arranged in alphabetical order. The names of the husbands of married females are enclosed in brackets:

No. Names. [Married Names.] Residence.

245. Aaron Baltimore, Md.
118. Aaron Bedminster, Pa.
207. Abraham Waynesboro, Pa.
86. Abraham Adams County, Pa.
101. Abraham New Salem, Ohio
143. Abraham Mickleys, Pa.
191. Abraham Fairfield, Pa.
240. Adam Voltaire, Pa.
165. Adeline Waterloo, N. Y.
412. Adam Voltaire, Pa.
371. Adelaide Waynesboro, Pa.
310. Albert Joseph Newport News, Va.
328. Albert Joseph Easton, Pa.
147. Alfred Thomas Mickleys, Pa.
395. Alice Funkstown, Pa.
171. Alice R [Richardson] Waterloo, N. Y.
313. Alice M [Newhard] Near Allentown, Pa.
431. Alberta Baltimore, Md.
316. Amanda M [Henninger] Near Ironton, Pa.
331. Amanda C [Hammersley] Allentown, Pa.
150. Amanda [Schadt] Ruchsville, Pa.
122. Amanda [White] Doylestown, Pa.
267. Americus Green Cashtown, Pa.
253. Amos Wesley Fairfield, Pa.
424. Axis R Roanoke, Ind.
40. Anna [Sheldon] Mickleys, Pa.
45. Anna [Wasser] Mickleys, Pa.
60. Anna [Deshler] Waterloo, N. Y.
72. Anna [Lutz] ___, Indiana
409. Anna M [Miller] Voltaire, Pa.
390. Anna Belle Gettysburg, Pa.

382. Annie [Myers] Table Rock, Pa.
374. Annie Waynesboro, Pa.
133. Anna Lovina Mickleys, Pa.
351. Annie E Seneca Falls, N. Y.
324. Annie S [Albright] Washington, D. C.
304. Annie D Mickleys, Pa.
296. Anna E Catasauqua, Pa.
263. Anna M [Wetzel] Fairfield, Pa.
250. Anna S Fairfield, Pa.
244. Anna M YorkCounty, Pa.
236. Annie Waynesboro, Pa.
194. Annie [Gordon] Franklin County, Pa.
153. Anna C [Sieger] Siegersville, Pa.
433. Anna Baltimore, Md.
453. Anna M Near Cashtown, Pa.
466. Annie E 210 Green street, Philadelphia, Pa.
477. Anna M Ruchsville, Pa.
448. Arthur Cashtown, Pa.
105. Augustus Cashtown, Pa.
268. Avilla [Wolff] Orrgleu, Pa.
414. Avilla York, Pa.
501. Arthur, P. J. St. Cloud, Minn.
5. Barbara Mickleys, Pa.
35. Barbara [Dieterly] Bedminster, Pa.
232. Bertie Waynesboro, Pa.
167. Bayard T Waterloo, N. Y.
442. Bertha B Sevens Stars, Pa.
455. Bertha K Cashtown, Pa.
299. Bessie C Catasauqua, Pa.
492. Blanch E Cashtown, Pa.
198. Blanch Waynesboro, Pa.

429. Carrie York, Pa.
297. Carrie E Catasauqua, Pa.
145. Carolines [Levan] Coplay, Pa.
341. Caroline [Paul] Allentown, Pa.
16. Catherine [Balliet] Shamokin, Pa.
21. Catherine [Biesecker] Adams County, Pa.
28. Catherine [Beisher] Bedminster, Pa.
43. Catherine [Seigfried] Lehigh County, Pa.
49. Catherine [Burkhalter] Clinton County, Ind.
70. Catherine [Miller] Cashtown, Pa.
129. Catherine A Allentown, Pa.
162. Catherine B Waterloo, N. Y.
199. Catherine [Bell] Waynesboro, Pa.
381. Catherine [Hartman] Mumasburg, Pa.
152. Catherine [Zeigler] Mechanicsville, Pa.
489. Calvin Seven Stars, Pa.
154. Carl M St. Cloud, Minn.
111. Charlotte [Donalson] Cashtown, Pa.
275. Charlotte [Thorn] Gettysburg, Pa.
246. Charlotte [Salterham] Mt. Royal, Pa.
56. Christina [Byle] Seigfrieds, Pa.
54. Charles Trexlertown, Pa.
64. Charles Waverly, Iowa
103. Charles Ortanna, Pa.
149. Charles Allentown, Pa.
255. Charles Belle Plain, Kansas
327. Charles F Allentown, Pa.
339. Charles H Allentown, Pa.
464. Charles L Philadelphia, Pa.
411. Charles Voltaire, Pa.
432. Charles Baltimore, Md.
260. Charles E Fairfield, Pa.
9. Christian Mickleys, Pa.
500. Clara G St. Cloud, Minn.
387. Clara [Rebert] Cashtown, Pa.
173. Clara B Waterloo, N. Y.
361. Clara Greencastle, Pa.
449. Clarice Cashtown, Pa.
447. Clarence Cashtown, Pa.
350. Clarence H Mansfield, Ohio

179. Cora LeMars, Iowa
291. Cora Margaret, Kansas
397. Cora A Columbus, Ohio.
440. Cora M Seven Stars, Pa.
454. Cora E Cashtown, Pa.
427. Cora Baltimore, Md.
334. Crisse D Ironton, Pa.

402. Daisy B Fairfield, Pa.
430. Daisy Baltimore, Md.
491. Daisy McKnightstown, Pa.
13. Daniel Greensboro, Pa.
24. Daniel Adams County, Pa.
76. Daniel Fairfield, Pa.
82. Daniel Waynesboro, Pa.
94. Daniel Cashtown, Pa.
117. Daniel Cashtown, Pa.
190. Daniel Fairfield, Pa.
206. Daniel Waynesboro, Pa.
362. Daniel. Harrisburg, Pa.
365. Daniel Waynesboro, Pa.
398. Daniel Columbus, Ohio
477. Daniel R Ruchsville, Pa.
78. David Ortanna, Pa.
148. David Ironton, Pa.
258. David A Fairfield, Pa.
385. David A Cashtown, Pa.
161. Delancy Seneca Falls, N. Y.
16S. Dewitt Waterloo, N. Y.
212. Dorothy R [Rebert] Cashtown, Pa.
62. Deborah [Fegley] Waterloo, N. Y.

295. Edgar C Catasauqua, Pa.
312. Edgar, M Philadelphia, Pa.
388. Edgar L Burkittsville, Md.
293. Edith R Catasauqua, Pa.
373. Edna Waynesboro, Pa.
494. Edna Cashtown, Pa.
163. Edson L Waterloo, N. Y.
61. Edward B Waterloo, N. Y.
242. Edward York, Pa.
349. Edward B Mansfield, Ohio
128. Edwin Mickleys, Pa.
321. Edwin A Mickleys, Pa.
473. Edwin A Ruchsville, Pa.
164. Edwin Waterloo, N. Y.
104. Eli Frederick, Md.

221. Eli Funkstown, Pa.
252. Elias F Perth, Kansas
272. Elliot P Cashtown, Pa.
438. Elmer E Perth, Kansas
437. Elma C Alburtis, Pa.
233. Ella Waynesboro, Pa.
478. Ella M Mickleys, Pa.
323. Ella C [Bieber] Kutztown, Pa.
233. Ellen J [Kugler] Easton, Pa.
290. Eleanora [Saunders] La Joya, New Mexico
470. Elizabeth G Philadelphia, Pa.
55. Elizabeth [Fahler] Allentown, Pa.
44. Elizabeth [Troxell] Allentown, Pa.
74. Elizabeth [Diehl] New Oxford, Pa.
92. Elizabeth [Walter] Virginia
110. Elizabeth [Trostle] Adams County, Pa.
205. Elizabeth [Stephy] Waynesboro, Pa.
193. Elizabeth Fairfield, Pa.
495. Elizabeth G Cashtown, Pa.
471. Elizabeth G Philadelphia, Pa.
170. Elsie L [Loveridge] Waterloo, N. Y.
141. Eliza A Mickleys, Pa.
130. Eliza [Kuntz] Nazareth, Pa.
403. Effie M Fairfield, Pa.
484. Edward Easton, Pa.
71. Eliza ___, Illinois
498. Edward G St. Cloud, Minn.
228. Emma [Shellman] Cashtown, Pa.
367. Emma Waynesboro, Pa.
393 Emma Funkstown, Pa.
178. Emma [Comine] Janesville, Iowa
408. Emma [Hinkle] Voltaire, Pa.
270. Emmaline a Cashtown, Pa.
189. Emma F; [Trostle] Fairfield, Pa.
113. Ephraim Adams County, Pa.
126. Ephraim Mickleys, Pa.
160. Erastus Seneca Falls, N. Y.
58. Esther [Troxell] Clinton County, Ind.
211. Esther [Hagerman] Cashtown, Pa.
284. Euphemia [Nicholas] Bedminster, Pa.
354. Eva Auburn, N. Y.
471. Eva H Ruchsville, Pa.

443. Eva G Seven Stars, Pa.
444. Fannie D Seven Stars, Pa.
182. Frances [Van Ordstrand] Waverly, Iowa
166. Frances E [Mosher] Seneca Falls, N. Y.
134. Francisca Mickleys, Pa.
345. Francis W Lincoln, Neb.
379. Frank New Salem, Ohio
439. Frank F Perth, Kansas
158. Franklin Waterloo, N. Y.
144. Franklin P Ballietsville, Pa.
346. Franklin B Seneca Falls, N. Y.
319. Franklin P Mickleys, Pa.
399. Franklin M Columbus, Ohio
347. Frederick Cleveland, Ohio
301. Frederick W Philadelphia, Pa.
172. Georgiaxna [Westbrook] Fayette, N. Y.
115. George Cashtown, Pa.
238. George Waynesboro, Pa.
401. George O Fairfield, Pa.
394. George Funkstown, Pa.
288. Granville Margaret, Kansas
435. Grant Denver, Col.
497. Gertrude York, Pa.
372. Grace Waynesboro, Pa.
445. Goldie M Syracuse, N. Y.
462. Guy Cashtown, Pa.
52. Hannah [Lugwig] Allentown, Pa.
108. Hannah Cashtown, Pa.
120. Hannah [Fackenthal] Doylestown, Pa.
151. Hannah [Wolf] Allentown, Pa.
137. Hannah [Benkert] London, England
224. Hannah M [Metz] Fairfield, Pa.
33. Hannah [Deiterly] Bedminister, Pa.
486. Harold Seneca Falls, N. Y.
234. Harriet [Bennett] Waynesboro, Pa.
215. Harriet [Hershy] Gettysburg, Pa.
81. Harriet [Pitzer] Ortanna, Pa.
186. Harriet R [Myers] Fairfield, Pa.
427. Harry York, Pa.
293. Harry T Catasauqua, Pa.

487. Harry W New Salem, Ohio
364. Harvey J Scottsdale, Pa.
426. Harry York, Pa.
286. Harvey Margaret, Kansas
174. Helena Waterloo, N. Y.
2S2. Helena Philadelphia, Pa.
475. Helen M Ruchsville, Pa.
330. Heinrich J Brainard, Minn.
4. Henry Whitehall, Pa.
11. Henry Mickleys, Pa.
84. Henry Seven Stars, Pa.
256. Henry Fairfield, Pa.
176. Henry Le Mars, Iowa
204. Henry Waynesboro, Pa.
135. Henry J Philadelphia, Pa.
311. Henry J Philadelphia, Pa.
159. Henry C Mansfield, Ohio
156. Henry L Hamburg, Pa.
352. Henry L Seneca Falls, N. Y.
359. Herbert W Jersey City, N. J.
77. Hester [Plank] Gettysburg, Pa.
88. Hester [Bushy] Hornstown, Pa.
219. Hiram Gettysburg, Pa.
326. Howard Ballietsville, Pa.
480. Howard L Mickleys, Pa.
177. Hudson Auburn, N. Y.
377. Henrietta [Mickley] Cashtown, Pa.
344. Henrietta [Nyce] Hamburg, Pa.

285. Ida E [Saunders] La Joya, New Mexico
318. Ida H [Breinig] Near Mickleys, Pa.
475. Ida M Ruchsville, Pa.
195. Ida [Cleek] Adams County, Pa.
483. Irwin Easton, Pa.
154. Isabella Trexlertown, Pa.
386. Issac Cashtown, Pa.
217. Israel Cashtown, Pa.
418. Israel R York, Pa.
481. Irene Coplay, Pa.
348. Irene E [Kern] Mansfield, Ohio

25. Jacob Adams County, Pa.
31. Jacob Bedminster, Pa.
38. Jacob Mickleys, Pa.
96. Jacob Florhs, Pa.
216. Jacob McKnightstown, Pa.

421. Jacob C Roanoke, Ind.
67. James Allentown, Pa.
85. James Adams County, Pa.
214. Tames Near Gettysburg, Pa.
223. James Fairfield, Pa.
482. James G Easton, Pa.
407. James R Fairfield, Pa.
127. James W Catasauqua, Pa.
300. James W Catasauqua, Pa.
132. Jane [Phillips] Pulaski City, Va.
184. Jane [Healy] Janesville, Iowa
405. Jane Fairfield, Pa.
227. Jane [Henry] Cashtown, Pa.
114. Jeremiah Adams County, Pa.
218. Jeremiah M Burkittsville, Md.
356. Jessie Fay Auburn, N. Y.
410. John Voltaire, Pa.
368. John Philadelphia, Pa.
73. John Fairfield, Pa.
18. John Adams County, Pa.
97. John Voltaire, Pa.
50. John Near Hokendauqua, Pa.
188. John Philadelphia, Pa.
209. John Waynesboro, Pa.
249. John York, Pa.
270. John A Cashtown, Pa.
420. John A Roanoke, Ind.
271. John A Cashtown, Pa.
298. John C Catasauqua, Pa.
438. John Joseph Perth, Kansas
1. John Jacob Mickleys, Pa.
8. John Jacob Mickleys, Pa.
138. John Jacob Visalia, Cal.
292. John Jacob Margaret, Kansas
307. John Jacob Mickleys, Pa.
342. John Heinbach Allentown, Pa.
460. John Oscar Cashtown, Pa.
2. John Martin Adams County, Pa.
3. John Peter Bedminster, Pa.
12. Joseph Franklin County, Pa.
41. Joseph Philadelphia, Pa.
53. Joseph Lehigh County, Pa.
140. Joseph P., U. S. N. Mickleys, Pa.
317. Joseph B Coplay, Pa.
422. Joseph E Roanoke, Ind.
120. Josiah Bedminster, Pa.

136. Josephine [Johnson] Philadelphia, Pa.
116. Julia [Wilson] Gettysburg, Pa.
23. Julia [Piper] Huntington County, Pa.
102. Kate [Comfort] Gettysburg, Pa.
467. Katie E Philadelphia, Pa.
363. Lavina [Smith] Waynesboro, Pa.
239. Lavina [Reiser] Hall, Pa.
266. Lemuel Syracuse, N. Y.
343. Lewis_ Hamburg, Pa.
500. Lewis J St, Cloud, Minn,
355. Le Roy Auburn, N. Y.
119. Levi O. Pipersville, Pa.
358. Lena M. Jersey City, N. J.
357. Lida Jersey City, N. J.
231. Lillie Waynesboro, Pa.
305. Lillie E [Chance] Wayne, Pa.
389. Lillie A [Shellenburger] Carlisle, Pa.
416. Laura [Stine] York County, Pa.
325. Laura [Hauck] Easton, Pa.
425. Louisa [Althen] York County, Pa.
279. Lucinda Bedminster, Pa.
376. Lucy A [Deardorff] Cashtown, Pa.
384. Lydia [Warren] McKnightstown, Pa.
287. Lycurgus Margaret, Kansas
247. Lucinda [Baublitz] Strincstown, Pa.

6. Magdalena [Deshler] Irish Settlement, Pa.
302. Mabel C Catasauqua, Pa.
213. Magdalena [Rebert] Cashtown, Pa.
59. Magdalena [Siegfried] Waterloo, N. Y.
46. Magdalena [Burkhalter] Lower Milford, Pa.
404. Maggie K Fairfield, Pa.
197. Margaret Waynesboro, Pa.
78. Margaret [Musseliman] Fairfield, Pa.
89. Margaret [Hake] York County, Pa.
235. Margaret [Pitzer] Waynesboro, Pa.

261. Margaret A [Donalson] Fairfield, Pa.
20. Margaret [Saeger] Allentown, Pa.
26. Maria M [Hecker] Allentown, Pa.
27. Maria [Snyder] _ Philadelphia, Pa.
262. Maria S [Stoops] Fairfield, Pa.
99. Maria [Comfort] Gettysburg, Pa.
146. Maria A Mickleys, Pa.
400. Marietta Columbus, Ohio
378. Marietta [Henry] Cashtown, Pa.
289. Mary Margaret, Kansas
369. Mary Waynesboro, Pa.
479. Marcus W Mickleys, Pa.
370. Marshall Waynesboro, Pa.
80. Martin Fairfield, Pa.
441. Mary A. Seven Stars, Pa.
458. Mary E Cashtown, Pa.
200. Mary [Bell] Waynesboro, Pa.
124. Mary [Weaver] Macungie, Pa.
407. Mary E [Lowers] Voltaire, Pa.
276. Mary E Cashtown, Pa.
183. Mary E [Newell] Janesville, Iowa
208. Mary A Waynesboro, Pa.
157. Mary A [Guth] Guths, Pa.
333. Mary A [Biery] Ironton, Pa.
393. Mary L Gettysburg, Pa.
48. Mary M [Snyder] Bloomsburg, Pa.
185. Mary M [Bomgarden] Fairfield, Pa.
27. Mary [Snyder] ___, Ohio
68. Mary A [Bell] Adams County, Pa.
37. Mary M [Moyer] Mercer County, Pa.
107. Mary M [Hentzleman] Cashtown, Pa.
281. Mary E [Sheetz] Philadelphia, Pa.
502. Mathias F St. Cloud, Minn.
237. Matilda [Little] Waynesboro, Pa.
461. Maud Cashtown, Pa.
353. Maud A. [Poulein] Washington, D. C.
493. Maud C. Cashtown, Pa.
220. Melinda [Cover] Gettysburg, Pa.
434. Melvin. Denver, Col.
273. Mervin O Cashtown, Pa.
457. Millie I Cashtown, Pa.
306. Minnie F Mickleys, Pa.
230. Minnie Waynesboro, Pa.
452. Mitchell S Cashtown, Pa.

380. Morgan. McKnightstown, Pa.

257. Naomi E [Ogden] Fairfield, Pa.
364. Nora Cashtown, Pa.
366. Nora Waynesboro, Pa.

314. Oscar F Ruchsville, Pa.

280. Pearson Philadelphia, Pa.
468. Pearson Philadelphia, Pa.
10. Peter Mickleys, Pa.
19. Peter Mickleys, Pa.
32. Peter Bedminster, Pa.
42. Peter Mickleys, Pa.
83. Peter Cashtown, Pa.
95. Peter Florhs, Pa.
123. Peter O Margaret, Kansas
203. Peter Green Castle, Pa.
226. Peter Fairfield, Pa.
315. Preston Mickleys, Pa.

303. Ralph C Catasauqua, Pa.
283. Reed Bedminster, Pa.
456. Robert E Cashtown, Pa.
446, Ronald E Syracuse, N. Y.
459. Roy A Cashtown, Pa.
259. Rebecca [Brown] Fairfield, Pa.
248. Rebecca [Braum] York, Pa.
229. Rebecca [Funt] Cashtown, Pa.
125. Rebecca [Thomas] Catasauqua, Pa.
109. Rebecca [Bercaw] Near Cashtown, Pa.
98, Rebecca [Hinman] Lancaster, Pa.
87. Rebecca [Bushy] Wyattsville, Pa.
196. Robert Waynesboro, Pa.

14. Sarah [Blumer] Allentown, Pa.
39. Sarah [Schwartz] Northampton County, Pa.
47. Sarah [Hass] Mercer County, Pa.
69. Sarah [Beisecker] Delphi, Ind.
75. Sarah [Plank] Gettysburg, Pa.
91. Sarah [Hereter] Gettysburg, Pa.
93. Sarah [Plank] Near Gettysburg, Pa.
110. Sarah J [Pettis] Near Cashtown, Pa.
139. Sarah [Wilson] Laramie, Wyoming
187. Sarah [Culp] Near Fairfield, Pa.

201. Sarah [Summers] Waynesboro, Pa.
241. Sarah York County, Pa.
254. Sarah S [Fuss] ___, Kansas
269. Sarah Frederick City, Md.
274. Sarah [Cover] McKnightstown, Pa.
320. Sarah J Mickleys, Pa.
336. Sarah A [Hammersly] Allentown, Pa.
415. Sarah J York, Pa.
419. Sallie M Gettysburg, Pa.
450. Sallie Cashtown, Pa.
488. Samuel J New Salem, Ohio
265. Samuel Orrglen, Pa.
465. Samuel A Philadelphia, Pa.
51. Salome [Troxell] Mechanicsville, Pa.
417. Savilla York, Pa.
375. Savilla [Sheely] Cashtown, Pa.
277. Sherry F. Cashtown, Pa.
413. Silas Voltaire, Pa.
210. Simon Waynesboro, Pa.
243. Solomon Roanoke, Ind.
451. Stella Cashtown, Pa.
308. Stella Alburtis, Pa.
65. Stephen Le Mars, Iowa
180. Stephen Buffalo, N. Y.
161. Stephen D. Seneca Falls, N. Y.
90. Susan [Arendt] Arendtsville, Pa.
7. Susanna. [Miller] Whitehall, Pa.
106. Susanna Near Cashtown, Pa.
169. Susan J Waterloo, N. Y.
202. Susan [Good] Waynesboro, Pa.
30. Susanna [Statzel] Philadelphia, Pa.
57. Susanna [Moyer] Lehigh County, Pa.
22. Susanna [Biery] Allentown, Pa.

66. Thomas Waverly, Iowa
142. Thomas Mickleys, Pa.
340. Thomas F Allentown, Pa.
423. Thomas E Roanoke, Ind.
469. Thomas E Philadelphia, Pa.
472. Thomas B Ruchsville, Pa.

250. Urias Denver, Col.
332. Urias D Ironton, Pa.

490. Virginia McKnightstown, Pa.

383. Virginia [Plank] McKnightstown, Pa.
436. Wesley A. Perth, Kansas
322. William J Mickleys, Pa.
192. William Fairfield, Pa.
63. William B Waterloo, N. Y.
338. William D Allentown, Pa.

222. William Columbus, Ohio
181. William Jersey City, N. J.
131. William J Alburtis, Pa.
496. Wilbur L Berkittsville, Va.
337. Winfield S Allentown, Pa.

360. Zillah Jersey City, N. J.

Index Second

The following index contains the names of those who have been united by marriage with the descendants of John Jacob Mickley, as far as they are recorded in the preceding catalogue. The place of residence is indicated as accurately as could be determined:

No. Names. Residence.

273. Adams, Catherine Cashtown, Pa.
324. Albright, James Washington, D. C.
63. Alleman, Sarah Waterloo, N. Y.
410. Aldinger, Kate Voltaire, Pa.
425. Althen, Fred York County, Pa.
90. Arendt, Israel Arendtsville, Pa.

9. Balliet, Paul Ballietsville, Pa.
16. Balliet, John Shamokin, Pa.
243. Baker, Elizabeth Roanoke, Ind.
71. Barkdsell, John ___, Illinois
247. Baublitz, Peter Strinestown, Pa.
28. Beisher, Jacob Bedminster, Pa.
68. Bell, George Adams County, Pa.
199. Bell, Jonas Waynesboro, Pa.
200. Bell, Daniel Waynesboro, Pa.
137. Benkert, George London, England
234. Bennett, Joseph Waynesboro, Pa.
109. Bercaw, Samuel Cashtown, Pa.
323. Bieber, Walter Kutztown, Pa.
6. Bieber, Michael Whitehall, Pa.
19. Biery, Rebecca D Mickleys, Pa.
18. Biery, Margaret Adams County, Pa.
333. Biery, John Ironton, Pa.
10. Biery, Salome. Mickleys, Pa.
22. Biery, Frederick Allentown, Pa.
100. Biesecker, Rebecca Fairfield, Pa.

21. Biesecker, Jacob Adams County, Pa.
69. Biesecker, John Delphi, Ind.
251. Biesecker, Margaret Denver, Col.
278. Blocher, Clara Cashtown, Pa.
14. Blumer, Henry Allentown, Pa.
41. Blumer, Diana Allentown, Pa.
339. Bohler, Sarah Allentown, Pa.
185. Bomgarden, Samuel Fairfield, Pa.
97. Boyer, Elizabeth Voltaire, Pa.
328. Bradcr, Emma Easton, Pa.
248. Braum, Peter. York, Pa.
318. Breinig, Oliver B. F Mickleys, Pa.
259. Brown, John D ___, ___
117. Bucher, Martha Cashtown, Pa.
—. Burkhalter, Elizabeth B. Mickleys, Pa.
11. Burkhalter, Mary M Mickleys, Pa.
343. Burkhalter, Barbara Hamburg, Pa.
46. Burkhalter, Charles Lower Milford, Pa.
49. Burkhalter, Daniel Clinton County, Ind.
87. Bushy, Henry Wyattsville, Pa.
88. Bushy, Nicholas Kornestown, Pa.
42. Butz, Anna Mickleys, Pa.
144. Butz, Sarah Ballietsville, Pa.
56. Byle, Peter Seigfrieds, Pa.

158. Callorn, Anna Waterloo, N. Y.
305. Chance, Dr. Henry M Wayne, Pa.
160. Clement, Margaret Seneca Falls, N. Y.
195. Cleek, Jacob Franklin County, Pa.
102. Comfort, Peter Gettysburg, Pa.
99. Comfort, Henry Gettysburg, Pa.
178. Comine, Joseph Janesville, Iowa
127. Cooper, Anna L Catasauqua, Pa.
220. Cover, Thomas Gettysburg, Pa.
274. Cover, William Gettysburg, Pa.
80. Crook, Anna Fairfield, Pa.
187. Culp, William Fairfield, Pa.

376. Deardorff, Daniel H Cashtown, Pa.
6. Deshler, Peter Whitehall, Pa.
15. Deshler, Joseph (?) Whitehall, Pa.
60. Deshler, John Waterloo, N. Y.
9. Deshler, Elizabeth Whitehall, Pa.
126. Deshler, Eliza Ann Mickleys, Pa.
120. Dieterly, Elizabeth Bedminster, Pa.
36. Dieterly, George. Bedminster, Pa.
33. Dierterly, Daniel Bedminster, Pa.
74. Diehl, George New Oxford, Pa.
261. Donaldson, John A Fairfield, Pa.
112. Donaldson, John. Cashtown, Pa.
241. Doll, Catherine. York, Pa.
154. Dorr, Augusta St. Cloud, Minn.
419. Dubbs, Jacob Roanoke, Ind.

280. Everhart, Mary Philadelphia, Pa.
123. Eckert, Lydia Ann Margaret, Kansas
143. Erdman, Maria Mickleys, Pa.
380. Erb, Mary McKnightstown, Pa.

120. Fackenthal, Jacob Doylestown, Pa.
55. Fahler, George Allentown, Pa.
62. Fegley, David. Waterloo, N. Y.
54. Fegley, Henrietta Near Mechanicsville, Pa.
128. Fogel, Matilda E Mickleys, Pa.
266. Ford, Ida F Syracuse, N. Y.
255. Forney, M Bell Plain, Kansas
24. Florh, Salome Adams County, Pa.
218. Fraine, Emily. Burkittsville, Md.

222. Fritz, Sarah Columbus, Ohio
64. Frantz, Sarah. Le Mars, Iowa
148. Frantz, Maria Ironton, Pa.
64. Frantz, Margaret Waverly, Iowa
177. Frink, Mary. Auburn, N. Y.
229. Funt, Grant Cashtown, Pa.
254. Fuss, Ezra ___, Kansas

161. Garlick, Harriet Seneca Falls, N. Y.
203. Gilbert, Margaret Green Castle, Pa.
202. Good, Daniel Waynesboro, Pa.
194. Gorden, George Franklin County, Pa.
272. Gorden, Millicent Cashtown, Pa.
245. Gladfelter, Rose Baltimore, Md.
266. Grimes, Margaret Adams County, Pa.
157. Guth, Moses Guths, Pa.
103. Green, Jane Ortanna, Pa.

211. Hagerman, George. Cashtown, Pa.
25. Hahn, Barbara. Adams County, Pa.
89. Hake, Peter York County, Pa.
336. Hammersley, James B Allentown, Pa.
73. Hantzleman, Harriet Fairchild, Pa.
107. Hantzleman, Daniel Cashtown, Pa.
12. Hartman, Eliza Franklin County, Pa.
381. Hartman, John Mumasburg, Pa.
47. Hass, John Lehigh County, Pa.
181. Hatfield, Kate Jersey City, N. J.
325. Hauck, Alvin Easton, Pa.
184. Healy, Homer Janesville, Iowa
26. Hecker, Jonas Allentown, Pa.
149. Heimbach, Eliza Allentown, Pa.
316. Henninger, Frank Ironton, Pa.
378. Henry, Dill Cashtown, Pa.
227. Henry, George Cashtown, Pa.
252. Herbert, Mary. Perth, Kansas
91. Heretor, Jacob Adams County, Pa.
83. Heretor, Anna Cashtown, Pa.
85. Hershy, Harriet Adams County, Pa.
214. Hershy, Mary Gettysburg, Pa.
215. Hershy, George Gettysburg, Pa.
408. Hinkle, B. F. Voltaire, Pa.
98. Hinman, John Lancaster, Pa.
41. Hopfeldt, Cordelia Philadelphia, Pa.

423. Hubley, Claudia Roanoke, Kansas

136. Johnson, John J. Philadelphia, Pa.
388. Karn, Hannah .Waynesboro, Pa.
3. Keck, Eva Bedminster, Pa.
131. Keck, Lucy Alburtis, Pa.
38. Kern, Anna Mickleys, Pa.
52. Kern, Joseph ___, ___
348. Kern, Rufus A Mansfield, Ohio
96. Knause, Mary Florhs, Pa.
326. Koch, Margaret Ballietsville, Pa.
317. Kohler, Laura. Coplay, Pa.
130. Kuntz, Rev. D. M Nazareth, Pa.
335. Kugler, John. Easton, Pa.
35. Kramer, Samuel Bedminster, Pa.

240. Laird, Hannah Voltaire, Pa.
145. Levan, Frances Coplay, Pa.
88. Lower, Conrad Hornestown, Pa.
379. Lohr, Sarah New Salem, Ohio
315. Long, Susan Mickleys, Pa.
170. Loveridge, Oliver P Waterloo, N. Y.
331. Lucas, Frank Catasauqua, Pa.
52. Ludwig, George Allentown, Pa.
138, Luther, Emma Lois Visalia, Cal.
71. Lutz, Benjamin ___, Ind.
222. Lilly, M Columbus, Ohio

224. Metz, Jesse Fairfield, Pa.
135. Majilton, Mary J Philadelphia, Pa.
267. Mickley, Henrietta Cashtown, Pa.
377. Mickley, Americus G Cashtown, Pa.
7. Miller, Andrew Whitehall, Pa.
1. Miller, Susane Mickleys, Pa.
53. Miller, Catherine Lehigh County, Pa.
66. Miller, Margaret Waverly, Iowa
180. Miller, Sarah Buffalo, N. Y.
70. Miller, Martin L Cashtown, Pa.
116. Miller, Jacob Gettysburg, Pa.
385. Minter, Sarah J Cashtown, Pa.
37. Moyer, Daniel Mercer County, Pa.
57. Moyer, Thomas Lehigh County, Pa.
158. Mountain, Mary Mansfield, Ohio
166. Mosher, William A Seneca Falls, N. Y.

219. Mundorff, Charlotte Gettysburg, Pa.
78. Mussleman, Christian Fairfield, Pa.
258. Mussleman, Sarah Fairfield, Pa.
95. Myers, Sarah Florhs, Pa.
103. Myers, Lydia New Salem, Ohio
186. Myers, Latimer Fairfield, Pa.
382. Myers, Robert Table Rock, Pa.

183. Newell, Daniel Janesville, Ohio
313. Newhard, M Near Allentown, Pa.
284. Nicholas, William S Bedminster, Pa.

34. Ott, Samuel Bedminster, Pa.
32. Ott, Mary Bedminster, Pa.
257. Ogden, Robert Fairfield, Pa.

341. Paul Nicholas Allentown, Pa.
110. Pettis, Samuel Cashtown, Pa.
132. Phillips, Enoch Pulaski City, Va.
23. Piper, John Huntington County, Pa.
81. Pitzer, Levi Ortanna, Pa.
235. Pitzer, Charles Waynesboro, Pa.
83. Pitzer, Rebecca Cashtown, Pa.
216. Pitzer, Eliza McKnightstown, Pa.
77. Plank. George Gettysburg, Pa.
75. Plank, George Gettysburg, Pa.
93. Plank, Abraham Gettysburg, Pa.
383. Plank, Harvey McKnightstown, Pa.
100. Polley, Harriet Fairfield, Pa.
353. Poullin, D. Edward Washington, D. C.

213. Rebert, James Cashtown, Pa.
387. Rebert, William M Cashtown, Pa.
212. Rebert, Joseph Cashtown, Pa.
84. Rebert, Elizabeth Seven Stars, Pa.
239. Reeser, Joseph Hall, Pa.
171. Richardson, Erastus J Waterloo, N. Y.
217. Rife, Elizabeth Cashtown, Pa.
84. Reynolds, Rebecca Fairfield, Pa.
221. Rook, Mary Funkstown, Pa.

20. Saeger, Jacob Allentown, Pa.
290. Saunders, John M La Joya, New Mexico

285. Saunders, Edwin La Joya, New Mexico
246. Satterham, Peter Mt. Royal, Pa.
314. Schadt, Jemima Ruchsville, Pa.
39. Schwartz, John Northampton County, Pa.
150. Shadt, Henry Ruchsville, Pa.
40. Sheldon, Andrew Mickleys, Pa.
188. Scott, Clara Philadelphia, Pa.
228. Shellman, George Cashtown, Pa.
375. Sheely, Jacob Cashtown, Pa.
281. Sheetz, William Philadelphia, Pa.
389. Shellenberger, Dr. Eph Carlisle, Pa.
94. Shull, Catherine Cashtown, Pa.
104. Shull, Elizabeth Frederick City, Md.
237. Settle (or Little), George Waynesboro, Pa.
84. Settle, Elizabeth. Seven Stars, Pa.
152. Sieger, John Siegersville, Pa.
43. Siegfried, Daniel Lehigh County, Pa.
59. Siegfried, Joseph Waterloo, N. Y.
363. Smith, Thomas Waynesboro, Pa.
147. Smith, Sarah Mickleys, Pa.
27. Snyder, George ___, Ohio
29. Snyder, Andrew Philadelphia, Pa.
48. Snyder, Daniel Bloomsburg, Pa.
30. Statzel, G. Henry Philadelphia, Pa.
14. Stein, Jacob Allentown, Pa.
2. Steckel, Catherine Adams County, Pa.
416. Steine, Paul W York, Pa.
205. Stephy, George Waynesboro, Pa.
207. Stephy, Sarah Waynesboro, Pa.
223. Singley, Elizabeth Fairfield, Pa.
262. Stoops. Daniel Fairfield, Pa.
407. Sowers, John Voltaire, Pa.
201. Summers, George Waynesboro, Pa.
204. Summers, Sarah Waynesboro, Pa.
105. Stover, Elizabeth Cashtown, Pa.

125. Thomas, Samuel Catasauqua, Pa.
275. Thorn, Charles Gettysburg, Pa.
111. Trostle, Peter Cashtown, Pa.
189. Trostle, John Fairfield, Pa.
386. Trostle, Ida. Cashtown, Pa.
51. Troxell, John Mechanicsville, Pa.
58. Troxell, Stephen Clinton County, Ind.

44. Troxell, Peter Allentown, Pa.
61, Troxell, Catherine Waterloo, N. Y.

182. Van Nordstrand, A Waverly, Iowa

92. Walter, Henry ___, Virginia
76. Walter, Elizabeth Fairfield, Pa.
384. Warren, Abraham McKnightstown, Pa.
45. Wasser, John Lehigh County, Pa.
124. Weaver, Valentine Macungie, Pa.
172. Westbrook, Isaac Fayette, N. Y.
263. Wetzel, John Fairfield, Pa.
116. White, James Gettysburg, Pa.
122. White, William Doylestown, Pa.
119. Worman, Lucy Ann Pipersville, Pa.
116. Wilson, John Gettysburg, Pa.
139. Wilson, William W Laramie City, Wyoming
151. Wolf, Ludwig Allentown, Pa.
268. Wolff, Rev. D. W Orrglen, Pa.

40. Youndt, John. Mickleys, Pa.

152. Zeigler, John Mechanicsville, Pa.
421. Zent, Cora Roanoke, Ind.

www.ingramcontent.com/pod-product-compliance
Lightning Source LLC
Chambersburg PA
CBHW032022040426
42448CB00006B/705